VALUE PUBLIC

THE ULTIMATE NFT GUIDE FOR BEGINNERS

A HANDBOOK ON INVESTING IN NON-FUNGIBLE TOKENS. EARN EXTRA MONEY AND GENERATE PASSIVE INCOME BY CREATING YOUR ART ON A BLOCKCHAIN.

ISBN: 978-84-19674-00-5

"Whereas most technologies tend to automate workers on the periphery doing menial tasks, blockchains automate away the center. Instead of putting the taxi driver out of a job, blockchain puts Uber out of a job and lets the taxi drivers work with the customer directly."

Vitalik Buterin

Free bonuses for our readers

Free bonus #1

Our Metaverse Guide 2023 will give you an excellent overview of the hottest decentralized Metaverse Projects. You will see the market capitalization of each project and which cryptocurrencies are funding each project that might explode in price in the future.

Free bonus #2

Never feel lost again if you read NFT posts and chats on social media!

Download our NFT Insider Glossary, where we list more than 200 terms and abbreviations that help you to dive into the NFT space much faster.

To get your bonuses go to

www.thevaluebird.com/bonus

Contents

Introduction

Since Bitcoin is in the financial news nearly every day, you probably already have a good idea of what it is. Chances are, you probably wish you'd learned more about Bitcoin and bought some nine years ago when the price was still around $100. This is exactly where we are now with NFTs or non-fungible tokens. You might have heard of non-fungible tokens already, but aren't sure what they are exactly.

"NFT" doesn't really sound sexy, but when you discover how they have attracted millions upon millions of dollars from investors and collectors since 2020, we know they'll grab your attention.

NFTs are more interesting than Bitcoin because of their many different applications that have the potential to transform our lives completely. And the technology for them is just at its beginning. There are many NFT use cases that we can't even imagine at the moment, but we assume that in ten years' time, the majority of people will have NFTs, and they will be common in our everyday lives. Just as we can't imagine a day without our smartphones anymore, we will not have a life without NFTs. That being said, ignoring this disruptive technology could be the most expensive decision you make in this decade!

Unfortunately, most people that have heard of NFTs think they are just funny, overpriced image files, but in fact, they are currently one of the most underestimated technologies out there. If you are a business owner, you can use NFT technology in your business. The use cases for NFTs are constantly growing, and businesses that use that technology will be miles ahead of their competition. Why? Because 99% of business owners don't know about NFTs and how they can use them. In this book, we will explain the details that will give you the first-mover advantage.

Now it is still early, and many people have never heard of NFTs. But why do you think so many global corporations are currently investigating how they can use and implement this technology for their benefit? From Amazon, Adidas, eBay, GameStop, Facebook, Instagram, and Nike to Twitter—they all want a slice of the growing NFT cake. This is because they know that this technology will play a major role in our future. After reading this book, you will gain a powerful advantage: you will be one step ahead of the majority of people who don't know about NFTs. You will discover how NFTs can make many jobs obsolete in the future while creating new income streams for those who adapt to this technology quickly. Continue reading so you can use the first-mover advantage for your life and business.

Have you heard of the digital NFT artist called Beeple? In March 2021, the auction house Christie's sold his piece *Everydays: The First 5000 Days* for a stunning price of $69.3 million. Stay with us—in a later chapter, we'll explain what led to such a high sales price of just one digital image. As an outsider, it might sound absurd, but once you understand the story behind it, you will get just as excited about it as everyone else.

Even though it might feel like others already grabbed insane profits from CryptoPunks and the Bored Ape Yacht Club, we assure you—you are not too late. The early bird catches the worm, and you are still early enough for non-fungible tokens!

This NFT handbook is here to help you build your nest in the new, exciting world of non-fungible tokens. Don't worry if you are not that tech-savvy, Value Bird will always bring you books written without repetitive technical jargon so that even NFT beginners will feel confident in the NFT world. We use simple language and easy-to-follow examples to guide you through everything you need to know about blockchain and NFT technology.

We worked on this book for months to give you all the knowledge you need to navigate the blockchain world and monetize your new-found knowledge in the next decades.

NFTs can be used to replace paper documentation, but also for trading many assets without any intermediary, ranging from art and collectibles, event tickets, virtual fashion, virtual land and real estate, in-game items, music albums, books, and so much more. We are just seeing the beginning here. In ten more years, we will be surrounded by NFT technology. Your car might have an NFT, for example, and each time it goes to a garage, its kilometers are documented on a blockchain so no one can't cheat anymore.

Not sure NFTS are worth your time? Think about it— NFTs can be worth a lot. A whole lot. Many investors right now are worried about rising inflation rates. NFTs are not necessarily affected by inflation, and they can help investors hold out during hard times like these. But how?

During an era of inflation, investors are looking for non-cash assets that preserve their value and so they push their money into those assets. They look for investments that can maintain a relative purchasing power compared to the US dollar. Digital art NFTs, like other forms of art, might retain their value regardless of inflation.

But NFTs can also be used by creatives and content creators. If you are a creative, you are likely familiar with not getting enough credit for your work. After selling your work to the buyer, your income stream or that piece is finished. You are no longer a part of any following resale of your work. If you know how to create and sell an NFT of your art, however, that doesn't have the be the case. And even if you have to sell your art, the copyrights can remain yours (depending on the license you sell it with). You can also configure royalties for your NFT, which means you will receive a commission every time your NFT finds a new owner. Passive income. Sweet, right?

If you wish to sell your art in the form of an NFT, you need to understand the basics and learn the language spoken in the NFT scene. In the beginning, most people do not understand what NFT experts are talking about. But fortunately, since you've got this book, you are only a few pages away from knowing all there is to know about NFTs, from their history to their uses and their advantages to their disadvantages.

NFTs have different use cases you probably don't know about—yet—and there are many more use cases on their way. The NFT journey has just started; we cannot even imagine all the areas of our lives they are going to change. With this book, you'll become acquainted with the current and potential use cases of NFTs, propelling you miles ahead of your neighbor or work colleague who hasn't even heard of them.

Don't worry, it is not too late to start. In fact, you're right in time. Now, you can get in at better prices and enjoy your future profits. Why? In 2022, the NFT market dropped drastically. Because of that, prices are low again, so it's a good time to sink your teeth in while the ignorant people are still scared. Businesses recognize this good timing too. Amazon is planning possible sales of NFTs in the future, GameStop plans to launch its own NFT marketplace, and eBay just acquired KnownOrigin, a UK-based NFT marketplace, in June 2022.

There is also the fact that social media giants like Facebook and Instagram may turn to an NFT marketplace where you will not only show off your NFTs but also buy and sell them for cryptocurrencies like Ethereum, Solana, or Polygon.

A study by German consulting agency Roland Berger concluded that tokenization of buying and selling of company shares could lead to gains of €4.6 billion by 2030. And it won't stop there.[1] The megatrend tokenization will have a strong impact on the whole financial industry for sure, and NFTs are the driving force behind that impact.

At the end of this book, you will not only be knowledgeable about NFTs, but you will also be able to use that knowledge to get your first ones. And, even possibly, have started making money from them already. You will understand the principles behind NFTs much better than before and their new, disruptive applications. You will also understand how to make your own NFTs, how to sell them, and where you can sell them.

If you are among the group of people who believe NFTs are scams, your doubts will dissolve by the end of this book (we'll cover that in chapter 8). We recommend genuine websites and blue chip NFT projects that are likely to preserve their value. We also write about typical scams that NFT beginners often fall for so you can identify and avoid them. Who knows, you could become the next owner of an NFT worth more than Beeple's *Everydays*.

This book provides all you need to know about NFTs. It serves as a one-stop resource for people interested in NFTs and those who want to profit from them. We not only tell you about NFTs and the technology behind them, but we also show you how to make your own in short, simple steps.

You will also learn how to create and sell those NFTs and how to invest in them. And lastly, we also show you the different strategies you can implement when selling your NFTs and how to be successful at it.

After we dabbled in other crypto projects, we explored NFTs and found that we thrived in this area. From our time spent researching crypto assets, understanding how they work, and making several investments, we were able to convert that knowledge into making profits. We've fine-tuned our process and are now helping others get into the NFT space using very easy steps.

There is no better time to start than now. Have fun while reading, and we hope you enjoy the book. We can't wait for the day when we'll be writing your NFT success story.

Chapter 1: Understanding the Blockchain Technology behind NFTs

Don't worry if you are new to non-fungible tokens. In this chapter, we will lay out the foundation for you, explain what non-fungible tokens are, and discuss how blockchain technology works. You might already have noticed the hype around selling digital art or collectible items as NFTs, but the application of NFTs has grown far beyond just being a video, music, or image file with the potential of soaring in price after a while. They have evolved, and they are going to evolve in the future. We believe we are just seeing the beginning of what is possible, just as we saw in the early 1990s with the beginning of the Internet.

It is getting more difficult to browse the Internet without coming across NFTs or crypto or the blockchain. There are more and more test trials for using NFTs in art, fashion, music, tickets for events, supply chains, real estate titles, videos, tacos, and even toilet paper. [2]

Tacos and toilet paper? Really? Yes. That's just how popular NFTs are these days. NFTs are selling faster than Dutch tulips from the seventeenth century. Faster than tickets for a Taylor Swift concert. Faster than your grandma's cookies at your grade school bake sale. Some are selling for millions of dollars in cryptocurrencies.

So, why do some sell for millions and others sell for pennies? Why are some NFTs so expensive? You are not the only one asking these questions. Are NFTs worth the hype, the money, or your time? Or are they just another pretty bubble soon to pop, as some financial experts believe? Once you understand how NFTs work you will be able to judge for yourself. You will also see why NFTs are an alternative investment and why every penny you invest in them may reward you in the future.

Before we look at what NFTs are, let's look at the technology behind non-fungible tokens—blockchain technology. Without understanding what a blockchain is, it will be difficult to fully comprehend NFTs.

What Is a blockchain?

Are you familiar with a database? Or have you ever come across a ledger before? That's simply what a blockchain is. But in the case of a blockchain, the ledger is distributed across a network of different computers or so-called network nodes.

But a blockchain is much more than a database. According to Investopedia, a blockchain can be seen as a distributed database or ledger shared among multiple computer network nodes. It is similar to a cashbook used for accounting, in which you write down all your income and expenses. This cashbook is copied thousands of times to many computers which makes it extremely safe. [3]

Blockchain technology is so innovative that it removes the need for third parties between buyers and sellers. Stockbrokers, attorneys, insurance agents, record labels, notaries, and ticket resellers—everyone who processes paperwork to help buyers and sellers execute transactions—are likely to be out of work in a few years when the governments start implementing this technology. Why? The blockchain offers security and guarantees that trust and fidelity are maintained.

How Does the Blockchain Work?

When a blockchain stores information, it stores it as a group. These groups of data are called blocks. The blocks in a blockchain hold specific information and have a definite storage capacity. The added information is mostly transaction records carried out by participants of the network. Still with us? Great.

The transactions are partially written using encryption techniques in the blockchain. At the same time, blockchains are also very transparent. Everyone can see each transaction in these public ledgers, the wallet addresses of the sender and receiver, and how much was transferred. Who owns a wallet address cannot be seen, however, and it does not allow anyone to access the wallets and submit or change entries. This is carried out automatically by program scripts and an automated transaction validation process. Participants of the network receive transaction fees or newly minted coins as a reward for their calculation work and stabilization of the network. Cool, right?

When the transactions are verified, the verification is conducted on a group of transactions, not a single transaction. This batch of transactions is known as a block. Each block has a defined storage capacity. Whenever a block is filled and all transactions have been verified and confirmed, the block of transactions is then appended to the previously verified block, creating a constantly growing chain: the blockchain. Each newly added block makes the whole data chain more secure because hackers would not only need to alter transaction data in one block but in many previous blocks as well.

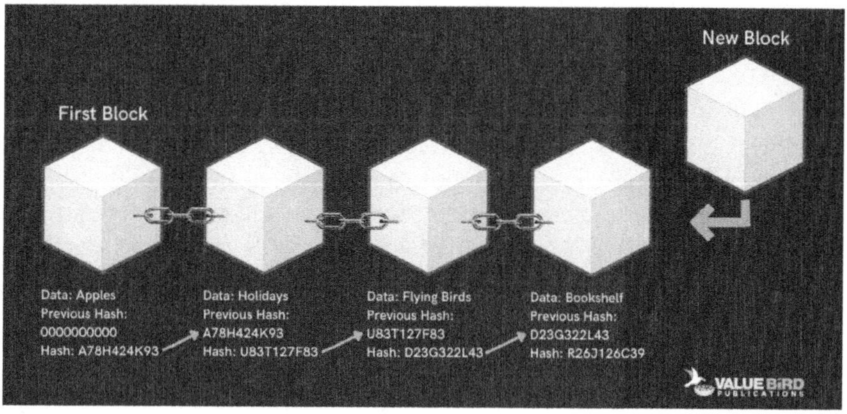

Image 1: Structure of a blockchain

When new transactions are performed on a blockchain, either bought, sold, or transferred, it is shared to the ledger of all the participants in the network. A blockchain can be seen as an extremely long digital accounting ledger shared across a network of many computers.

One of the main goals of the blockchain is to make digital information immutable. That is, store, record, and distribute information digitally without it being edited or even deleted by any of the participants of the computer network.

In contrast to the blockchain, information in a central database is structured in tables that can be modified. The data in a blockchain, however, can't be changed or reversed. Only new data can be added since each block added to the chain has a unique timestamp and cryptographic signatures known as hashes.

The concept of blockchain technology first came in 1991, however, its use case started to become popular in 2009. You may have heard of it, it's a little thing we call the Bitcoin blockchain.

But since then, the use of blockchain technology has constantly evolved and exploded. It is not only used for Bitcoin, but it has supported the rise of other cryptocurrencies, the emergence of smart contracts, and the widespread use of non-fungible tokens. There are also decentralized finance (DeFi) and decentralized applications (DApps). Understanding these before jumping into NFTs will help you get a broader and better understanding of what they are.

Every participant in the network manages the ledger through a so-called "consensus mechanism." If one block in the blockchain changes, every participant in the network would be aware of the change and reject a transaction. If hackers want to hack the blockchain, it is extremely difficult, because the data is not stored on a central computer, but decentral. The weakness where hackers can steal cryptocurrencies is rather not the blockchain itself, but the wallets and exchange accounts of cryptocurrency owners. But don't worry, we will come back to those scenarios in chapter 9, where we explain easily avoidable common security mistakes.

Decentralized Nature of Blockchains

Aside from being secured, decentralization is another good characteristic of blockchain technology, making it very popular today. By being decentralized, the blockchain has no central location where things are stored. It also has no central authority, no administrator, no government, or any other body overseeing how it operates. Depending on how popular a blockchain is, there are multiple, even thousands, of copies of the blockchain spread on many computers in different locations worldwide. A different person maintains each copy. Each one of the computers in the network is referred to as a node. All nodes are constantly syncing with each other to maintain the integrity of the transaction data.

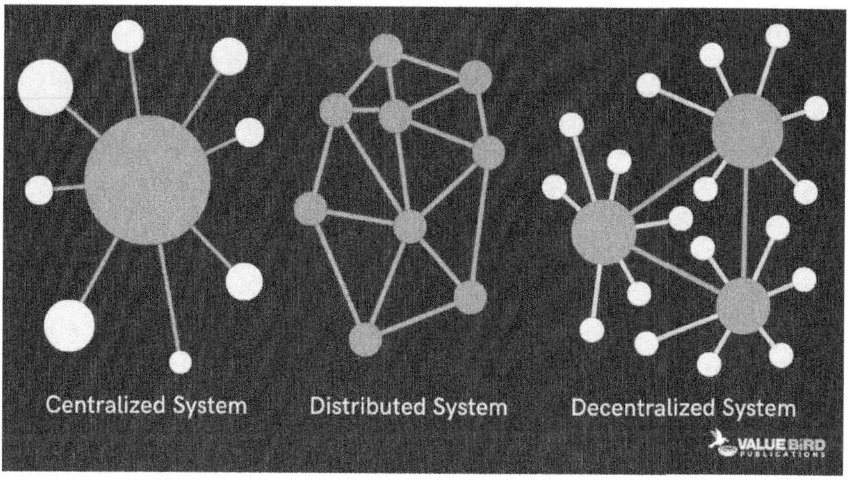

Image 2: Dentralized & Decentralized Systems

Miners or validators earn (or win) the right to validate transactions in a block. This is determined by the proof-of-work or proof-of-stake method, which we'll discuss later in this chapter.

Let's take, for instance, a company's server that has over 5,000 nodes of computers. The computers store information or use a database containing all the company employees' details, accounts, and even information about their clients. But this database is located in a particular location, say a warehouse, where the database can be operated from. Of course, there will be tight security to ensure maximum safety, and it wouldn't be in a place where it can be easily located. Nevertheless, it stands out as a weak point for that company. Imagine, what would happen if that warehouse lost electricity or Internet or if someone with a shady agenda decided to erase all that important information? Heck, what if the whole thing just burst into flames?

These are some of the problems of centralization that the blockchain does not have. This is because there are always several duplicates on different computers that are constantly being updated. In fact, not having these problems is one of the main reasons boosting blockchain technology's emergence and widespread use.

If the company's database was on a blockchain, its information would be distributed to several computers in different parts of the world. This would make that information more secure. Warehouse burns to the ground? No problem.

True, this would create redundancy, but it would ensure the fidelity of the information stored on it is always maintained. And even if someone with an evil intention tries anything malicious from their own end, it does not alter the node of the other participants. This makes their whole attempt futile.

For instance, on the Bitcoin blockchain, if such a thing were to happen, the entire network cross-checks with each other till they find the node with the wrong information. The punishment for this is very great, even though doing it would take a whole lot of energy. You'll find out more when we talk about the Proof of Work (PoW) and Proof of Stake (PoS) Consensus Mechanism.

Many measures are out in place to achieve this level of security and decentralization. In the blockchain, new blocks are added chronologically and linearly. They always come at the end of the chain. And to alter a change in it, the majority of the participants must agree to it. Aside from that, it is also challenging to do because of the hash, a cryptographic signature.

Each new block has a hash, a timestamp (as we mentioned above), and the hash of the information block before it. These hash codes are generated by mathematical functions which create strings of letters and numbers from digital information. An alteration in the block information will alter the hash codes as well.

Remember how we said hacking the blockchain will be very difficult? Well, this is why. When a hacker attempts to alter the chain to embezzle crypto from the other network participants, they will need to change a piece of block information. The information on that particular chain will not match that of the other participants, causing the chain to be considered illegitimate by the other participants. So, if the hacker wants to successfully carry out their ill act, it would be only possible if someone owns more than 50% of the network. Hence, it discourages hackers from attempting to hack the network. Hackers could only insert an altered blockchain in a so-called "51% attack" to make changes to transactions that have not been confirmed yet by the blockchain. A transaction is successful when six confirmations have been completed. Mind you, such a hack would require lots of computational power and hence, a lot of money, since the hacker would need the majority of the blockchain to pull off a successful hack like this.

Blockchains with smaller numbers of network participants have been attacked by 51% attacks. However, Bitcoin and Ethereum are very large networks and make it nearly impossible to be successfully attacked due to the high costs of acquiring 51% of the hashrate.

Many crypto blockchains are vast and quickly growing. This further makes the situation more challenging for hackers and safer for investors and blockchain users. When network participants notice such an event, all they have to do is hard fork or shift to a new and better version of the network. This would ultimately make the hacker's efforts useless and less rewarding. On the flip side, partaking in the blockchain is much more beneficial than attacking it.

The blockchain decentralized system is in place to ensure that transparency is upheld, and things go as planned. It ensures that the history of a block and the information stored on it can't be changed or reversed. It also helps in the validation of new blocks of record. When a block is filled, it is closed and attached to the previous block. But before this can happen, the blockchain decentralized network must agree. This agreement is done using the Proof of Work or Proof of Stake mechanism since no particular computer node is in control.

At first, blockchain was mainly thought of to hold crypto transaction records. But like every other type of technology, it has evolved. This technology can be used to store information like the stock inventory of a company, contracts between different parties, identification, and more.

Large corporations are very interested in blockchain technology for their logistic chains and product liability, for example. Each step in the supply chain from the raw materials and the manufacturing processes to the end product could be documented in a blockchain and therefore make the whole manufacturing process transparent and traceable. The question is, however, if complete transparency is really always in the interest of the manufacturer.

The blockchain might seem very complex but has limitless potential. It gives users more privacy and security, lower fees, and fewer errors. And as outstanding as it is, it is not without its shortcomings. Before looking at its pitfalls or cons, let's look at the pros of the blockchain.

Pros

- Removes human errors and increases accuracy
- Reduces cost of transaction by eliminating the need for a trusted third party
- Is immutable and can't be tampered with because it's decentralized
- Is very secure, efficient, and offers robust privacy for the participants
- Is very transparent
- Provides more secure alternatives for financial services in countries with underdeveloped and unstable governments.

As you can see, the blockchain is chock-full of pros, but nothing is without its downsides. Here are some of its cons.

Cons

- Mining is costly and often requires special hardware
- A history of illegal activities
- Issues with regulations
- Limitations with scalability

The blockchain has different applications that are being explored and improved with the growing technological advancement. A massive part of this is because of the increasing use of cryptocurrencies and Bitcoin.

For most investors, these are pretty big buzzwords. In mid-2022, there has been an increasing proliferation of non-fungible tokens and digital assets tokenization. So you can argue that the blockchain is dynamic and not static, and with its rate of evolution, there is no telling what the next decade will hold.

NFTs benefit greatly from the advantages of their underlying blockchain technology and its decentralized design. Let's look at the advantages and disadvantages of a decentralized system in the new Web3 (we'll explain this more later).

No Single Point of Failure

Even though banks have several locations, they've used centralized systems up to now to document all their transactions. A bank controls via one central authority its own database and verifies all transactions coming in and going out for all accounts held at the bank. The problem with a centralized system occurs when a hacker is able to gain access to all of the records in the database and either steal data or alter data records. This happened in 2019 when hacker Paige Thompson who was working for Amazon Cloud Services (AWS) obtained the personal data of more than 100 million Capital One bank accounts.[4] Since there was only one location for the complete data, the damage was huge. With a decentralized system, the total data can be spread on different servers and there is usually no way to download or alter the complete database. A hacker might access one of the Bitcoin nodes and alter previous transactions, but the other nodes will recognize these modifications and reject them.

No Single Controlling Authority

Banks, as an example again, are single, controlling authorities and are also subject to certain government regulations. A bank has full control of its database and how it is managed. Additionally, the bank has full control over all its customer's transactions. Do you have a check that you want to deposit? The bank determines the length of time for putting it on hold until it is credited to your account. Good luck trying to get those funds sooner. With a decentralized system, all transactions are verified and processed in the same manner. This means you are not depending on the decisions of a controlling authority and have 100 percent total control of your funds. Only you, and no one else, can do anything with your money (assuming that you have the private key to your wallet).

Transaction Speed

Let's say someone in the United States wants to send money to someone in Spain. They send a check via snail mail which would take many days to arrive and additional time to credit the check at the local Spanish bank. A much quicker method would be to use a bank transfer via the international SWIFT system. This would take about two to three business days to arrive. But since there are no paper notes involved and everything is already digital, isn't it strange it takes so long? Additionally, you are being charged an annoyingly high transfer fee for this slow transaction. Using a cryptocurrency such as Bitcoin or Ethereum, the exact same amount can be sent in 10 - 60 minutes (depending on the current transaction volume). Other cryptocurrencies such as Litecoin or Polygon can even carry out the transaction in a few seconds, and the fees are likely a fraction of what your bank will charge you.

Inflation Resistance

The central banks in each country are responsible for maintaining the value of the currency and issuing new money. All fiat currencies are backed by nothing—no gold, no silver, no other commodity. Just the full faith of every citizen. As with any fiat currency, the supply can be continuously increased by printing more money. Are Bitcoin and gold becoming more expensive? Or is the dollar simply losing more and more of its value? These are important questions. Bitcoin has a limited supply that maxes out at 21 million. Once that amount has been reached, no more will be minted. Ethereum, however, has no maximum supply defined. Each NFT usually (but not always) has a supply of 1, which is also its maximum supply.

Anonymity

Many people believe crypto wallets provide anonymity because you transact on the blockchain without any name or address. But is this really the case? When you use a crypto exchange such as Coinbase or Binance, you have to verify your identity at the last stage in the transfer process. Also, the European Union is pushing laws for the identification of every wallet holder or the holder's transactions will be blocked.[5] Sooner or later, we assume this will be implemented worldwide so that people can no longer hide their money from tax authorities. Above all, everyone can see any transaction or the holdings for every wallet address in a blockchain explorer. All your transaction history is written on the blockchain. Forever. And if you want to exchange your Bitcoins back into your local fiat currency, you have to identify yourself at one of the exchanges. Not particularly anonymous, is it? There are ways to stay anonymous on the blockchain, but they are inconvenient and beyond the scope of this book.

What are Cryptocurrencies?

Cryptocurrencies or cryptos are virtual or digital currencies secured by a cryptographic system, making it impossible to spend them more than once or counterfeit them.

Most cryptos are decentralized, and each type is based on a particular blockchain. Since a central authority does not control these currencies, they are void of government manipulation and interference and do not need an intermediary.

You can mine (= earn) cryptocurrencies by serving as a node validator or—much easier—buy them from exchanges. But it's quite rare to use them for transactions between a retailer and a consumer. Why is that? Isn't cryptocurrency supposed to be a means of exchange? Yes, you are right, they are. But depending on where you live, how modern the government is, and what the banking and tax system there is like, they are more or less accepted in B2C payments. El Salvador and the Central African Republic (CAR) are the only countries as of 2022 that have approved Bitcoin as legal tender, but most central banks all over the world are currently working on CBDCs (central bank digital currencies), which will be also new cryptocurrencies pegged to the value of a country's fiat currency. CBDCs will, however, be issued and managed by a central authority, the central bank, and they are therefore not decentral and will have a couple of other disadvantages as well. We will cover this topic in depth in our crypto book, but one key takeaway here is that blockchain technology will be the future of our financial system.

Cryptocurrencies like Bitcoin and Tether have found popular uses in international and cross-border transactions that would impact Western Union and MoneyGram. International transactions of large amounts have been quite difficult, expensive, and slow using traditional currencies.

Invented by Satoshi Nakamoto (an anonymous person) in 2008, Bitcoin has established itself as the biggest cryptocurrency holding the biggest market capitalization of all cryptos available, followed by Ethereum. On the website www.coinmarketcap.com, you can see the 10,000 most popular cryptos, links to their official websites, their market cap, circulating supply, the latest prices, and their price history.

Bitcoin has often been compared to gold, while Ethereum is called the silver of cryptos. Real silver is a metal to store value, but it is also an industrial metal because of its excellent electrical conductivity. Silver is used in soldering and brazing alloys, batteries, LED chips, medicine equipment, nuclear reactors, photography, solar panels, semiconductors, touch screens, water purification, and more. However, gold stores more value per weight than silver and has fewer industrial uses. This is the same for Bitcoin and Ethereum. While one Bitcoin can store a large value like a piece of gold and has few other use cases, Ethereum is cheaper but has many use cases. By the way, the symbol for Ethereum (ETH) looks like this:

Or Ξ

Each cryptocurrency should have something unique to bring to the table. There are more than 20,000 cryptocurrencies in use at the moment. Far too many in our opinion, and we will explain the most relevant cryptos for NFTs in chapter 7 and of course in full detail in our book about cryptocurrencies.

The Difference Between Coins and Tokens

After cryptocurrencies, the next thing you should know about is tokens. Talking about cryptocurrencies, people often use the terms coin and token interchangeably, which is incorrect because there is an important difference between the two. Cryptocurrencies that have their own blockchains, such as Bitcoin, Ethereum, or Ripple, are coins. Altcoins are any coins that are not Bitcoin (alternative to Bitcoin coins).

Tokens are cryptocurrencies that don't have their own blockchain but utilize another coin's blockchain. For example, Ethereum enables via smart contracts to create, issue, and manage tokens. Tokens are a derivative of the primary blockchain. Each blockchain uses its own smart contract. The smart contract for **fungible tokens** (= anything that is not unique) of Ethereum uses the Ethereum Request for Comment 20 (ERC-20) protocol. The stable coin Tether (USDT) is a popular (fungible) token that piggybacks on the Ethereum blockchain using the ERC-20 standard. Tether can be sent to any Ethereum wallet address, but not to a Bitcoin or Ripple wallet address.

What Is a Stable Coin?

A stable coin is a coin that has a fixed value to another asset, usually to the US dollar, euro, or gold. For example, the value for Tether (USDT) is always close to $1. **Do not invest long-term into a stable coin**, since it never increases in value, but rather inflates in value the same way that pegged FIAT currency does. All CBDCs (central bank digital currencies) will be a stable coin.

Millions of Transactions Every Day

Because many tokens (USDT, BNB, Dai, and Shiba Inu, to name a few) use the very popular Ethereum blockchain. In fact, Ethereum has far more daily transactions than Bitcoin. Ethereum is processing more than a million transactions every day on its blockchain:

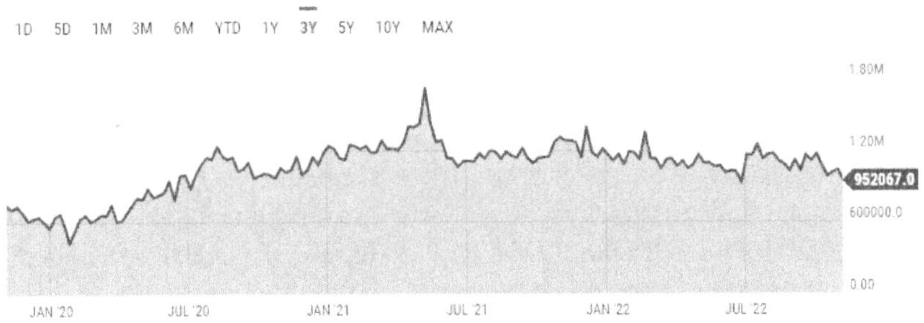

Image 3: Transactions per day on the Ethereum blockchain (by ychart.com)[6]

For the Bitcoin blockchain, the number of daily transactions are between 200,000 and 400,000 approximately:

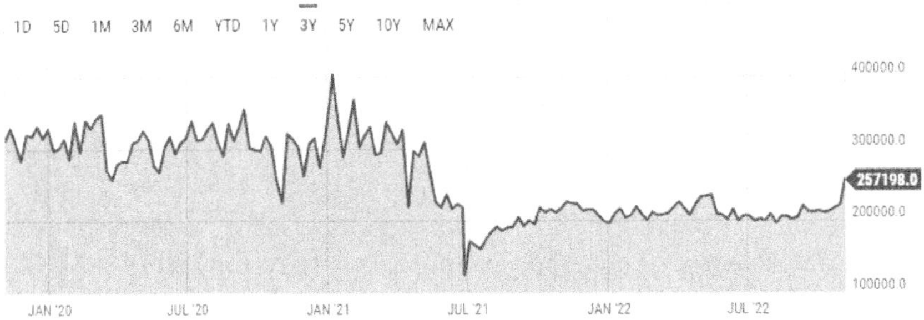

Image 4: Transactions per day on the Bitcoin blockchain (by ychart.com)[7]

The term "token" in "non-fungible token" (NFT) is a token that exists on a blockchain, but is not a native blockchain itself. Currently, most NFTs are created and sit on the Ethereum blockchain, but there are also other blockchains for NFTs such as Binance Smart Chain and Wax that we will describe in Chapters 7.

What are Smart Contracts?

One of the recent evolutions of the blockchain is smart contracts, which have led to more security, faster transactions, and better accuracy for buyers and sellers. It shows investors that what they are putting their money in is worthy of their trust, giving investors assurance to carry on. They have opened a new era of legal binding between two parties and might soon take over the mainstream legal world. But what are they, and how do they affect your understanding of NFTs?

Smart contracts are computer codes that act like agreements between two or more parties and consist of terms to be reached for the agreement to be fulfilled. Once these terms are reached, the agreement is complete, and the contract ends. Everything happens automatically. No need for human intervention, hence, no chance of error.

The beauty of smart contracts is that they are on the blockchain. Because they are there, they are faster in executing transactions and eliminate the need for the manual processing of documents. The contracts are made online, so the parties involved can be from different countries.

Smart contracts are a lot better than traditional, offline ones. Apart from being self-executing, they are trustworthy and dependable. Being on the blockchain means they are decentralized and immutable, increasing investors' confidence. And hey, you don't have to worry about a third party such as a notary when dealing with smart contracts. In fact, you also don't have to meet the other party one on one. We believe that future buying and selling of real estate, stocks, and equity will be processed by smart contracts and NFTs.

The smart contract that documents ownership and allows the transfer of ownership easily is the most important part of the NFT. Most people think NFTs are just funny, overpriced image files. However, smart contracts make NFTs the most underestimated technology out there today. The use cases in everyday business (and not just in a metaverse) are endless. And as we said in the introduction, businesses that use that technology will be miles ahead of their competition. Why? Because 99% of business owners don't know about NFTs and how they can use them.

Fractional Ownership

Smart contracts play a vital role in fractional ownership. Fractional ownership simply means that more than one person shares ownership of an item. The cost of an asset is split between individual shareholders so that they own fractions (or a percentage) of an item or an asset. This is not a new investment approach but has been around for decades.

Fractional ownership is made possible by smart contracts. How? The fractions of the objects need to have value. To do that, they need to become tokens. We already discovered that tokens are a derivative of the primary blockchain. To turn the fractions of an object into tokens, you need smart contracts. The smart contract splits the unique NFT (ERC-721) token into multiple fractions in the form of fungible ERC-20 tokens. The NFT owner outlines the number of ERC-20 tokens that will be created, their price, metadata, and other properties. Each fraction, or ERC-20 token, represents partial ownership of the entire NFT for a fixed price.

Let's say an investor wants to acquire a large hotel building, but he or she doesn't have all the money needed to buy it. A solution could be to tokenize the legal ownership into 10 tokens and sell it to 10 fractional owners. Each token holder will own 1/10 of the value of the hotel and the profit that it generates every year will flow back in equal parts to the investors. The main investor could acquire 5 tokens (= 50% of the hotel ownership) and the rest could be held by 5 other investors, holding 1 token each). It's not only more exciting but also a more accessible form of investment. If one investor wants to sell his fraction (= token), it could be achieved very quickly through a blockchain transaction, thanks to smart contracts. The annual profit will then flow into the new NFT owner's wallet.

Expensive NFTs could also be sold in fractions to several buyers. High-priced CryptoPunks, Bored Apes or Autoglyphs can become accessible again for fans that cannot afford one of these anymore. When an NFT is fractionalized, it becomes a tradable token whose value is directly tied to the value of its parent NFT.

But how do you interact with smart contracts? You need DApps! What are those? Let's find out.

How Decentralized Applications and Organizations Build the New Web3

The Internet has evolved drastically since its beginning, and it is still evolving. Currently, the trending buzzword is "web 3.0," or Web3, which is supposed to be a type of Internet based on public blockchains. It is, at the moment, rather a concept than a finished, working system. Let's look at the Internet's evolution briefly to understand where it will lead in the future:

- Web 1.0 was mostly about reading: the rise of search engines, read-only websites, and sending emails.
- Web 2.0 is about writing and creating: Users are encouraged to create content on social media such as Facebook, Snapchat, Twitter, etc., but the ownership of the user's content still belongs to Facebook, for example, and they store it centrally in their databases. Also, the use of smartphones became mainstream. You log in to websites via a username and a password. You need to remember a lot of usernames and passwords.
- Web 3.0 is all about ownership and decentralization. Users are supposed to have ownership of digital items and sections of the Internet and central authorities don't get to decide who gets to access what services. The metaverse will become popular, and certain websites will be only accessible if you connect your wallet and have a certain NFT in it. This is all currently in development.

To run a Web3, programmers are developing so-called DApps. Decentralized applications or DApps are like normal apps and offer similar functions, but they no longer run on a single server or store data centrally. Instead, they are built on blockchains and therefore on a decentralized network of numerous peer-to-peer network nodes. Their data is public, and they are using smart contracts. DApps should not have downtimes, because there is no single server that could go offline. Web3 will rely heavily on non-fungible tokens (NFTs), cryptocurrencies, and other blockchain entities.

DApps are usually open-source software applications, and their beauty lies in that no single authority controls these apps. And they are made for various applications. They can be used for surfing the Internet, accessing your social media sites, or even decentralized finance. To get an overview of what DApps are available, you can go to dappradar.com. Interesting examples of DApps are the trading card game Splinterlands (splinterlands.com), the music app Audius (audius.co), and the Binance Smart Chain token exchange PancakeSwap (pancakeswap.finance).

Parallel to the development of decentralized apps are often decentralized autonomous organizations (DAO) created that determine the development of a DApp or a project. DAOs are a new form of legal structure that are coming to prominence with no central governing body. DAOs are used to manage an entity similar to a corporation and to make transparent decisions within a project in a bottoms-up management approach by a collection of individuals instead of a central board of directors. DAOs rely heavily on—you probably guessed it already—smart contracts, which set the rules for the DAO. Members of a DAO can vote on a blockchain for certain decisions. To become a member of a DAO you usually have to acquire a special Token of that DAO. The more tokens you will hold, the more influence you can have on a project. For example, you can vote to implement a certain code to increase the circulating supply, burn a select amount of reserve tokens, or issue select rewards to existing token holders. Bitcoin is generally considered to be the first fully functional DAO.

As much potential as a decentralized organizational structure seems to have to replace some traditional companies, they also have their limitations. For starters, decision making through public votes may take longer than decisions by a CEO because people are all over the world in different time zones. Discussing a change within a community may take longer than actually implementing the change. Security is always a risk as well because a DAO requires significant technical expertise to implement. And finally, the treasury reserves of the DAO could be stolen, and wallets emptied. But bear in mind, this is all in a very early stage. With every hack, each possible security gap will be closed, and the technology will improve. We still remember how often we cussed after our computer crashed on Microsoft Windows 3.0 because we forgot to click on the "save" button during the last five hours of our work. Since Windows XP—like it or not—Windows runs pretty stably and Office apps are autosaving your documents.

Proof of Stake and Proof of Work Consensus Mechanisms

There are different mechanisms used to validate transactions on a blockchain that are carried out by the network nodes, which, if you remember, are computers on which special software for the network runs and that store a complete copy of the distributed ledger. Network nodes are responsible for the correctness and reliability of storing the entered data in the distributed ledger. The node or the so-called "validator" must determine if the address sending the cryptocurrency actually has that amount of cryptocurrency to send.

This is done by going backward in the chain: the sending address received the cryptocurrency from wallet D, which received it from wallet C, which received it from wallet B, and so forth, back to the latest verified block, which, in effect, validates the transaction all the way to the first block of the blockchain. By setting up a network node, you receive a small income from the transactions that go through your computer. Another nice way to make a little cash.

Once you understand the difference between how the two consensus mechanisms for validation and verification of a block work, you will also understand the difference between mining and minting. What are mining and minting? Let's take a look.

Most but not all cryptocurrencies are created from mining. Mining is the process where cryptocurrencies such as Bitcoin are generated by recording and verifying transactions on a public blockchain. In order to do so, computers with very high operational power solve very tedious mathematical equations and problems and in return are rewarded with fresh cryptocurrency. This complicated calculation process prevents hacking but happens at a low speed with a high cost for electricity consumption. The process for mining is called "Proof of Work" (PoW) and it serves two purposes: to create new coins as rewards for mining work and to maintain a record of all existing token transactions.[8]

Minting is a similar but different algorithm that is also referred to as "Staking." Minting uses the Proof of Stake (PoS) mechanisms to validate transactions and new blocks on a blockchain. In this, you don't have to worry about mining or solving complex problems. You just have to stake your cryptos, which means holding them to validate and earn validation rewards. It's not simple, but it's definitely not as hard as mining. Once your assets are staked, they are locked, where they help to provide liquidity for a particular set period. During these times, you'll earn rewards. The higher the assets staked, the higher the rewards.

The Proof of Stake mechanism is much faster than PoW as no complicated cryptographic puzzles have to be solved, but the main disadvantage is that it requires an often-enormous initial investment as well as a fairly high level of technical knowledge. You must purchase enough of the native token of that cryptocurrency to qualify as a validator. For instance, to participate as a validator for the Ethereum blockchain, you must stake 32 ETH (depending on the fiat exchange rate this could be anywhere between $32,000–$128,000) into the deposit contract and run three separate pieces of software: an execution client, a consensus client, and a validator.[9] When cryptocurrencies rise in market value, this problem could become worse. Only wealthy people can buy a network stake, or a group of people must create a staking pool. There is the danger of slowly reducing the decentralized structure of a cryptocurrency because the network will concentrate more on larger nodes.

Now, since you have learned the basics of the underlying technology of NFTs, which is blockchain technology, you are ready to dive deeper into the sea of non-fungible tokens.

Chapter 2: What are NFTs?

NFTs or non-fungible tokens are digital assets that are secured with cryptographic signatures and exist on a blockchain. It is basically a programming code for a smart contract. NFTs have special metadata and ID codes that differentiate them. Some of the metadata is mandatory and other is optional that can be added. NFTs are not like cryptocurrencies. They cannot be exchanged or traded at equivalency. This is because NFTs are not fungible, meaning they are not identical and can't be used for commercial transaction purposes.

Remember the Ethereum ERC-20 standard that applies to fungible tokens? There is also an Ethereum ERC-721 standard, which is important because it is the standard for the basis for non-fungible tokens. The standard defines the details of an NFT's ownership, its safety, and the metadata necessary for distributing and exchanging the tokens. Another, newer Ethereum standard, ERC-1155, has been developed by the team behind the Enjin project. The advantage of this standard is the allowance of batch transfers of NFTs—multiple assets on a single smart contract can be minted and transferred at once resulting in needing to pay the blockchain transaction fees only once. With the ERC-721 standard, however, if one were to transfer or mint multiple NFTs, each NFT would require a single transaction and therefore pay exorbitantly high transaction fees on Ethereum.

Because there are clear standards, different wallets and marketplaces are able to handle NFTs on the Ethereum network and Ethereum is currently the most popular blockchain for NFTs.

What is Fungibility?

Fungibility is when two different items have the same specification or properties, and the same individual units are interchangeable. That is, they are of the same value and worth the same. Some fungible items include common shares, commodities, cryptocurrencies such as Bitcoin and Ethereum, gold, bullion, barrels of oil, and even the dollar bill. Speaking of cryptocurrencies being fungible, not all crypto assets are. For instance, non-fungible tokens are not fungible because they are unique and cannot be interchanged. Let's imagine this scenario to truly understand the concept of fungibility and non-fungibility.

An employer gives $100 to an employee who promises to return it at a fixed date. On the due date, the employee will repay the employer $100, whether it was the same $100 bill the employer gave or not. That's to say, the two $100 bills can be substituted for the other. Another way around this is that the employee can repay a $50 bill, two $20 bills, and one $10 bill instead of just a $100 bill. The other four bills sum up to $100. This is possible because the dollar bill, like other fiat currencies, is fungible and is easily interchangeable.

Over to non-fungibility: imagine, instead of $100, an employer lends a black BMW 5 series car to an employee for an errand. After some time, a pink Ford Focus is returned. Do you think that is acceptable? Unless the employer loves pink sedans, of course, it isn't. If it's not the same car given out, nothing can replace it. That's non-fungibility. You could also not exchange a Rembrandt for a Monet. Both are unique, original, and non-replaceable.

Some other non-fungible or non-replaceable items you'll be familiar with are diamonds, real estate, land, baseball cards, and your wife or your husband (hopefully). Diamonds, for instance, can differ in size, cut, grade, and color. Houses have different needs for repairs and have special qualities, even if they are just the house's view or the little garden out back. It's the same for land. Different plots, mineral resources, textures, soils, and so on give each piece its own value. And just try to replace your wife or your husband. That's a whole different type of problem.

Bitcoins or $100 in your bank account can be divided and then reassembled together to create another fungible item of the same value, while non-fungible items cannot. The latter come whole and stay that way because they are indivisible and unique.

While fungible and non-fungible can look like opposites, the line between them is very thin sometimes. For instance, one ounce of gold is interchangeable with another ounce, making gold fungible, whether it was made by American Eagle, Degussa, Krugerrand, or Umicore. But there are cases where this is not obtainable, like very rare gold bars or coins. This can occur when gold that is expected or supposed to be fungible is given a serial number, like in the Federal Reserve Bank of New York case. By adding these identification numbers, one ounce of gold with a unique number is not the same or interchangeable with another, which makes gold, at that point, non-fungible.

A non-fungible token works like a cryptocurrency token, but usually with the maximum supply of one. Bitcoin has a limited supply of 21 million coins, which are all interchangeable, and you can break down each Bitcoin into many smaller units. The cryptocurrency token Tether, which is pegged to the US dollar, has no maximum supply. Just as fiat currencies such as the US dollar or the euro have no limit. The supply of the dollar can be inflated at any time by printing more dollars (or creating more virtually in the computer system of banks). The value of each dollar decreases of course when more is printed if we assume the demand remains more or less the same.

Since the supply of NFTs is usually one, it is unique and non-fungible. You cannot exchange one NFT for another as you could with a one-dollar note, because each NFT is different and a unique unit of data. You can compare an NFT with an original painting—there is only one. And on the blockchain, everyone can see the supply.

Technically, it is possible to mint identical copies of an NFT, for example, 100 or 1000. Each of these tokens can be exchanged freely because they would be the same—it would be one NFT of 100 tokens. This is just like you can buy limited edition prints of the same photo, each signed by the artist and sequentially marked. Of course, the more original copies exist, the lower the price of each will be.

If you look at the popular limited edition Bored Ape Yacht Club, there were 10,000 NFTs minted. Each has its own number #1234 in that collection and is therefore unique. If you look at the OSF's Red Lite District collection on the popular NFT marketplace OpenSea, you will see 210 identical images, and each is individually marked from #1/210 to #210/210. In this example, it is number 54 of 210 NFTs:

Red Lite District #54/210

It is astonishing how much people are willing to pay for the Red-Light District; however, the Red Lite District NFT number 54 is still a unique token with a supply of one, which makes it an NFT. Each token was minted separately to number each sequentially. If it would have a supply of more than one, you could not mark it sequentially. It would be a multitoken and all 210 tokens would have been created in one minting process. In fact, a multitoken of 210 would not be non-fungible anymore since they are identical and you can interchange them, but with a limited supply.

Be aware that editions can have different values. With traditional art prints, the highest value usually has the first edition of a print series (usually edition 1 of 500). In the NFT market, however, this is not always the case.

Ex-CEO of Twitter and Square, Jack Dorsey, sold his first tweet as an NFT for over $2.9 million, which he donated to charity. You can see this tweet for free in your browser: www.twitter.com/jack/status/20. But you will never own that tweet the same way the buyer owns it, even if you make hundreds of screenshots.[10]

If you go to the Louvre in Paris to take a photo of one of the most valuable paintings in the world, the Mona Lisa, that doesn't mean you own it. Strangely, this is what happens when people right-click and save a computer image on a website. Have you ever wondered why the Mona Lisa is invaluable? Could it be its uniqueness?

More examples of fungible and non-fungible assets are:

	Non-Digital	Digital
Fungible Bulk Goods	Fiat Currencies Precious Metals Standard Stamps Concert Tickets	Cryptocurrencies Apple Stocks Mutual Funds
Non-fungible unique items	Trading Cards Real Estate Blue Mauritius stamp Handmade Jewelry Airplane Tickets	Non-Fungible Tokens (for example Crypto Punks, Beeple's Everydays: the First 5000 Days)

VALUE BIRD PUBLICATIONS

Image 5: Examples of fungible and non-fungible assets

Choose The Right Types of NFTs

In the next chapter, we'll look more at popular use cases for NFTs followed by ideas of NFT applications for the future. You might be surprised how wide the range actually is. The use cases for NFTs are endless. But for now, here are a few.

Digital Collectibles

Digital Collectibles or digital art is usually created—you guessed it—digitally and is supposed to stay digital. They are either unique items or a limited-edition copy of a virtual item. The advantage of digital collectibles is that you do not have to store them (in a vacuum bag, under your mattress, in a vault behind a painting, etc.) and maintain them. The risk of damaging a digital collectible and the cost of ownership is practically zero.

Usually, they have a visual element such as digital art, a video clip, or a digital trading card. They are like physical collectibles, such as rare stamps or football cards, but exist only in digital format.

The CryptoKitties video game heralded the usage of NFTs as collectibles. It is regarded as the first time NFTs were used. In 2017, collectors fell over themselves to own CryptoKitties, distinct digital kittens. The CryptoKitties became so famous that you were not considered a serious collector if you did not have one.

Digital art or collectibles usually have one of the following forms:

- Images / animated GIFs
- Videos
- Audio
- 3D models
- books and texts

Images

Most of these NFTs contain a still image, such as Doodle, CryptoPunks, or Bored Ape Yacht Club collection. The image could be scanned images, digitally taken photos, images created on a computer, or a mix of all of these categories. With NFTs, there is no limit to file size or resolution, but each marketplace may apply a limit when minting the NFT. Always aim to offer high-resolution images to allow your audience to display them on a larger screen if desired.

An image can be either raster images (as known as bitmaps) or vector graphics. Raster images are composed of individual, tiny square pixels of color and have typical file formats .jpg, .gif, .tiff, or .png. All photos taken with a smartphone or digital camera are raster images because they can contain more color depth and color gradients than vector images. They have two disadvantages, however, one being that if you enlarge them, they will look pixelated and you can see the raster, and the other is that the file size is bigger than those for vector images.

Vector graphics on the other hand use mathematical formulas for paths to draw lines and curves between various points and store the color code for each shape (vector). Every color change would require a new shape to be created. The advantage of this is that vector images can be infinitely scaled up to any size without losing image quality. They are excellent for logos, illustrations, engravings, and embroidery. Typical file formats are .svg or .ai and the file sizes are generally smaller, too.

Image 6 Raster and Vector image comparison[11]

Before you buy an NFT, check what format and resolution it will come in, because sometimes the resolution is actually no bigger than what you see and download via a right mouse click on OpenSea. Large resolution is better than small so the image can be displayed on large screens.

Apart from avatars and profile images that represent certain identities in the webspace, memes are also popular NFT images. What is a meme? It's a piece of information, a joke or a jingle, which gets passed around a lot. Memes naturally self-replicate by being shared on social media. Why? Well, because we humans like to share and repeat stuff. When we repeat the joke or sing the jingle, we reproduce the meme.[12] Saint Hoax is a popular meme creator on Instagram with more than 3 million followers. (www.instagram.com/sainthoax) Memes have made millions of dollars as NFTs, confirming that making others laugh could be tremendously profitable. NFT memes will undoubtedly grow in popularity in 2022, as individuals seek new, imaginative, and unique methods to make money.

Videos

Another popular content format for NFTs is videos. For example, the NBA Top Shots NFTs contain highlight videos of moments in NBA history, and they are selling quite well. Videos don't have to be film content, it could also be a piece of digital art or static image with animated content, as it is in NFT trading cards of former American Football player Rob Gronkowski (gronknft.com). The card automatically flips over so you can see more information "on the back" of the card.

Most video formats won't repeat (except for animated .gifs), but NFT marketplaces like OpenSea will show them in a loop on the marketplace. If you use animated gifs on OpenSea, which are basically a sequence of still images, the thumbnail will automatically play the image sequence in the collections page as you can see, for example, in the Red Lite District Collection. A standard .mp4 format video would appear in the thumbnails as a static image, but play when you go to the NFT detail page. GIF files have two disadvantages because they are older technologies: The colors used are limited to 256 colors, which makes them less suitable if you want to offer a high-quality video, and they also have no audio. For better video quality, audio video file formats such as .mp4 are preferred, at least in HD quality.

The best NFT artists usually align the last frames with the first ones to create a seamless loop, especially when showing rotation objects. Seamless loops are more aesthetic to viewers—something to consider when creating your own NFTs.

Audio

An NFT can also contain a single song, an album, or even a music video. With this technology, musicians could go directly to their fans and sell unique, tokenized versions of their artwork, ideally yielding substantially higher profits. If more artists would use Web3 marketplaces instead of web2 platforms, it would cut out Spotify, Amazon Music, and Apple Music, the companies that currently make all the money. To earn $1 from one of these music giants, a music file has to be streamed between 140 to 250 times on one of these major platforms. And there is no transparency if the tracking of the streaming is really 100% correct. The global music industry is a multi-billion revenue industry, but artists only receive a small percentage of it. It is time to shift the whole industry and implement new models and payment options to reward creators for their work. What is currently missing, in our opinion, from the user perspective is an easy-to-use Web3 decentralized NFT music player or streaming service where you can play all of your music. The marketplaces that currently exist have only a small choice for streaming. We see the Audius platform (www.audius.co) going in the right direction, though.

Future NFT holders of songs might even earn money from holding music tokens in their wallets. NFT music artist 3LAU announced that he was forging an NFT music platform called Royal (royal.io), which will enable token owners to secure royalties from a musician's songs. 3LAU is one of the early adopters of music NFTs, selling his first NFT in 2020. In February 2021, he raised approximately $11.7 million with his Ultraviolet NFT album containing 33 different NFTs. What is even more surprising, he sold all of his NFTs in an auction that was just three days long. He admitted he was shocked by how successful the sale was.[13]

The buyer of an NFT album could also have exclusive rights, which would be similar to an album copy signed with a personal message by the artist.

We recommend offering your music to your audience in .wav files, which are uncompressed and have higher audio quality than the compressed .mp3 format. Also, prepare a preview image for the marketplace that you want to sell as the "album cover."

3D Models

3D models can represent a real-world or a virtual object. 3D models are often used in the industry for product designs, but also in augmented reality, games, and architecture. They became more popular among digital artists in recent years. With special headsets, you can view the model, move it, and zoom in and out. With a 3D printer, you can also create a physical model. In chapter 4, we have listed a marketplace that specializes in 3D model NFTs. On the marketplace itself, you will just see a 2D image, but you will get access to the .obj file after the purchase. Owners of the .obj file can import the model into most animation or modeling software and use the model (often an avatar) in a virtual world or video games. In the future, many metaverses will allow you to upload your 3D model file and use the object or avatar in that metaverse.

Gaming

The video game market is growing and growing. For in-game items such as weapons, armor, and skins, non-fungible tokens are booming and they are, pardon the pun, literally a game-changer in this industry. In the future, gamers will be able to earn money from playing games and reselling their in-game items to new, impatient gamers who want to gear up quickly and save hours of playing to earn their desired objects. And game developers can earn more money from in-game sales and every resale on the secondary market as well. For rare items that are no longer available in the game, prices could soar to $100,000. In the future, you will be able to trade NFTs on all gaming consoles, too.

Be aware that there are also many scammers out there trying to sell non-existing in-game items. There is also the risk that you pay a lot of money for a rare item, and once the game developers notice, they create hundreds of the same item. Therefore, we recommend not holding on to an in-game item for long and instead just quickly reselling it. By our knowledge, the best NFT games are currently Axie Infinity, The Sandbox, Gods Unchained, DeFi Kingdoms, Splinterlands, Sorare: Fantasy Football, Star Atlas, Parallel, Alien Worlds, Illuvium, Spider Tanks, DOGAMÍ, and The Walking Dead: Empires. Also watch out for a game called "Otherside," which the creators of the Bored Ape Yacht Club, Yuga Labs, are also currently working on.

Mobile gaming giant Zynga games is also going to explore blockchain gaming options. Zynga announced plans to expand their blockchain gaming team from the current 15 people to as many as 100 in February 2022.[14] If you are a developer, entering the NFT gaming system could be the best option for monetizing your creations.

CEO of Outlier Ventures Jamie Burke said, "people spend five times more in a blockchain game than in a conventional game." The reason for this is "that if the gamer can exit the game and cash out with crypto, and if they're free to do whatever the hell they want with the money, then they'll spend more money." This was proven by the game Axie Infinity, which is just the beginning of a much larger boom in gaming that is coming in the next decade.[15]

And what if you own the actual game itself? Well, only the owner truly owns the game and can play it, so it's all yours.

Fashion

Many global fashion brands are already investigating how they can use NFTs to build brand awareness, attract public attention, strengthen customer relationships, increase sales, and unlock new cash streams. This is digital fashion you can carry in style on your device, even if you can't wear it physically. Hundreds of high-end fashion companies are queuing up to create merchandise for the popular and exclusive Bored Ape Yacht Club community. And items sell out within hours. We think virtual fashion wearables are just scratching the surface. NFTs could create new ways to monetize and invest in fashion. The fashion industry is also queuing up at game developers to bring their digital wearables as NFTs into games. Burberry already launched the game Blankos Block Party, and Karl Lagerfeld is building its own NFT community and marketplace. Prada, Louis Vuitton, Mercedes-Benz, and Cartier founded their Aura Blockchain Consortium in April 2021 (auraluxuryblockchain.com) to create their vision of a global blockchain solution for all luxury brands that is easy to use for consumers.

However, a great share of NFT fashion is meant to be shown in a virtual world (metaverse) or worn by gaming avatars as a form of self-expression. Depending on the game, wearables might even enhance your avatar's abilities.

And lots of big-name brands are getting involved. In December 2021,

Nike bought a digital clothing creator called RTFKT. Dolce & Gabbana has sold its most expensive suit ever—The Glass Suit—for about $1 million (351384 ETH). Domenico Dolce and Stefano Gabbana designed the suit themselves.[16]

Textbooks

A new upcoming use case for NFTs will be textbooks. Yes, plain text can also be an NFT. Currently, authors do not participate at all from the secondary market after they sell their books to the first buyers. NFT technology will allow publishers and authors to collect royalties for every resale. This would add a fantastic new income stream for authors and also help customers quickly and easily sell the books they don't want to keep. Currently, Kindle eBooks cannot be resold because readers only purchased a license to read the book on their devices; they cannot give it to charity or a friend. Because of this limitation, we often don't mind paying a bit more to buy paperback books instead of kindle books. They take up space, but at least we can give away valuable information to friends and neighbors or sell it at a flea market.

Virtual Land / Real Estate

In recent virtual life and game projects, the creators offer virtual land for sale that only exists in that virtual environment. However, this land can have real-world value. Popular virtual worlds that offer NFT land sales are Decentraland, Sandbox, and Bloktopia. Decentraland is a virtual world that simulates the real world in which users can interact through their avatars. Avatars are customized representations of the participant. Investors acquire land here in the hope they can flip it later for a higher price or build something on it to monetize it. NFTs are the perfect technology to sell and transfer virtual land since the ownership and existence of the land are verified on a blockchain. You can buy virtual land on the project's respective marketplace or, for Sandbox and Decentraland, you can also find them on the most popular NFT marketplace OpenSea.

Digital lands have (similar to real estate deeds) a description of a specific location. Instead of being registered in the local land registry office, the information of all owners and transfers is stored on a blockchain.

NFT land buyers hope that buying virtual land now is similar to buying land in Miami 150 years ago while the city is being built and developed. The highest land sale price achieved so far in The Sandbox was $4.3 million.

Event Tickets

Event tickets are another use case of NFTs. However, we do not see strong demand for a secondary market here after the event has taken place. Some advantages of selling NFT tickets are that it could come with some digital art, prevent fake tickets, and the artist can cut out the middlemen such as Ticketmaster, CTS Eventim, or Eventbrite. Fake tickets are more common than you might think—according to CNBC, about 12% of all tickets sold in the US are fake.[17]

With NFTs, you can end ticket fraud, and artists and event organizers can also profit from each resale of a ticket, or if desired, a resale can be prohibited in the smart contract. After the event, the ticket becomes invalid, but it still stays in the wallet and may have a little collectible value.

The benefit of NFT event tickets seems more on the event organizers' side than on the consumer side. NFT tickets can be a useful marketing tool for customer loyalty and engagement, however. The ticket issuer could give a bonus if a customer has bought and attended more than 10 events, such as free food and drinks. For ticket buyers, it might also be easier to sell a ticket quickly online if, say, your impulsive little sister suddenly announces her wedding on the day of the event.

Blockchain Domain Names

Blockchain domain names are different from regular top-level Internet domain names such as **www.thevaluebird.com** The top-level domains are managed and controlled by a centralized authority called ICANN.

When we talk about blockchain domain names, we mean a simplified, user-friendly name for typical long and complicated wallet addresses. The blockchain domain address will be an NFT held in a cryptocurrency wallet, and you can sell it to other users via marketplaces such as OpenSea.

A bitcoin address has usually 34 characters, while an Ethereum address will have 42 characters, for example:

0xa66598f4D91275E50AeFf9CEea9c92dF5d2Ae0A2

With a blockchain domain, you can send money to this address using a simple valuebird.nft if valuebird.nft was previously associated with the wallet address. If you want to give someone your wallet address, you can just send your simple blockchain domain name instead of the long, cryptic address. There are two main players where you can register blockchain domains: Unstoppable Domains (unstoppabledomains.com) or Ethereum Name Service (app.ens.domains) for domains that end on .eth. Once you have minted your domain, you can configure on both domain-hosting websites all the different wallet addresses you need to receive different cryptocurrencies (Bitcoin, Litecoin, etc.). On the MetaMask wallet, you cannot receive Bitcoins, for example, so we suggest you get a Bitcoin wallet address from another wallet. After configuring your different wallets you can test sending the smallest possible amounts ($5–$10) to your blockchain domain address. Even if your blockchain domain ends in .eth, you will be able to receive Bitcoins once you have linked a Bitcoin wallet in the configuration page of your domain host.

In the future, there will be new decentralized browsers that can direct you via the blockchain address (for example: valuebird.nft) to a decentralized, blockchain-based website that cannot be controlled centrally or censored by the ICANN organization.

You usually pay the price for a blockchain domain only once, while a top-level domain you have to pay for annually. The price for a popular top-level domain can give you really nice profits. Early Internet users who secured common word domains such as insurance.com sold it for $35.6 million; hotels.com was sold for $11 million and shoes.com for $9 million. Blockchain domains are currently in the early adoption phase and will probably go mainstream later as top-level domains did.

More Types and Use Cases of NFTs

There are also other types of NFTs apart from the ones mentioned above. Financial products, insurance, and real estate titles will be booming in the world of NFTs. We predict that even online courses will involve NFTs. As long as you have the online course NFT in your wallet, you can log in and study. After you have finished your online course, you can resell your course and the course creator will receive a commission every time access is sold again.

As we've said before, NFTs will likely be everywhere. It is possible that the government will issue your ID card as an NFT, for example, or your new Patek Philippe watch will come with an NFT to prove its authenticity and link you to a loyalty program.

Could NFTs be used within the election system? For sure. Each voter would receive their own unique, digital ID, and because NFTs are secure, no one could possibly create any fake votes within the system. NFT technology could eliminate potential voting fraud.

We also expect most social media posts to be NFTs: Twitter tweets, Facebook statuses, Snapchat stories, Instagram Reels, or TikToks.

IBM has started to mint patents as non-fungible tokens on their own blockchain in partnership with the patent market platform IPwe. The tokenization of intellectual property makes it easier to license, commercialize, and potentially trade.[18]

Collaterals and Investments

In this book we mainly focus on digital art and rarities, but we would like to mention that there are also decentralized finance (DeFi) products such as NFT-backed loans. DeFi and NFTs have a common infrastructure. Because some DeFi apps will let you use your Bitcoins, Ethereum, or valuable NFTs as collateral for loans in Fiat currency, such as the US dollar, euro, or British pound. You need money and you have a valuable CryptoPunk NFT, but you don't want to sell it. A solution could be to use this precious NFT as collateral on a marketplace to receive 30% of its market value as a loan in FIAT currency.

In the future, you would have a real house title as an NFT, and you could use that one as collateral for a new loan to buy a small apartment. Once your luxury car comes with an NFT attached to it, you might be able to use its NFT to borrow some money short term as well.

Why Do NFTs Have Value and Why Are They So Important?

Since the Internet is easily accessible to more and more people, everything is slowly transforming into digital means. It started with letters and postcards, books, music, and videos, and is slowly reaching currencies, financial services, and many more aspects of our lives. Since everything is quickly becoming digital, there seems to be a need to replicate the property of real and rare physical assets. Fewer people are staying attached to the material world. If you ever have moved houses, you can guess how nice it would be to have your belongings on a computer rather than in stacks of boxes. People are packrats, we like to collect—stamps, shoes, Kinder Surprise figures, dolls, Starbucks coffee mugs, comic books, kitchen magnets, you name it. The market for collectibles is huge. Currently, many people associate NFTs with profile pictures of monkeys, cats, and dogs. But NFTs are more and bigger than that. Everyone will have some sort of NFT in the future. It will become part of our lives just as the Internet became part of our lives.

NFTs have huge potential to transform many established processes. For example, in the future, record labels will release music through NFTs instead of the traditional way. And they won't need agencies and intermediaries; they can fund their music through royalties from their fans. And for other artists, this is revolutionary, too. You actually don't need a physical object anymore. Many NFTs exist as digital art only. So you don't need to print, pack, and ship a photo anymore.

Non-fungible tokens can be used for several purposes, not only for arts. In the future, you might save your money for the notary when you buy a house or apartment. In the art market, it is revolutionary, because you can always look up when a piece of art was sold and for what price. Creators of fine art will not be dependent on galleries to exhibit and sell their paintings. Artists can communicate directly with their clients instead of going through agents and relying on their mercy. These things have not possible in the traditional art market. Since NFTs hold a smart contract on a blockchain, there is no need for middlemen or trusted intermediaries anymore. As we mentioned in the introduction, people who help buyers and sellers execute transactions are likely to be out of work in the future.

You may have heard about NFTs fairly recently, but they have been around as far back as 2015. So, why are they only just becoming popular?

Their rise in popularity can be traced to the fact that cryptocurrencies and blockchains are becoming adopted by many. And, apparently, the younger generation that grew up with smartphones as extensions of their bodies don't mind owning and investing in specialized content.

The value of an NFT depends on how popular it is. If you acquire a non-fungible token, you own the content. However, the content can still be online. The more people see it, the more popular it becomes. The more popular it becomes, the more its value increases.

The current method of revenue sharing when an asset is sold is pretty straightforward. The seller owns most of the revenue, but the creator will get a ten percent share and the platform gets a small percentage for its service. This creates a continuous revenue stream as more people buy and resell the digital asset.

If digital assets are to be sold and resold, they must be distinct and authentic. But how do we distinguish or even verify a valuable digital collectible from a cheap imitation? This is where blockchain technology comes in. With the help of blockchain technology, the unique information in digital assets that differentiates them from any other can be readily verified. The technology also prevents the proliferation of knockoffs because every digital asset is unique and has the imprint of the issuer, making it easier to trace the assets back to the creator.

Every other day news about NFTs appears in the media. Whether it's a celebrity issuing or acquiring a digital collectible or a digital asset worth insane money, NFTs are now making headlines. But is this enough to make NFTs mainstream? We think so. The future of NFTs looks bright since they are a type of proof of ownership. Instant proof of ownership will be the key to widely applying NFTs.

As we talked about previously, NFTs can also digitally represent tangible assets, such as event tickets or real estate. We strongly believe that with technological advancement, integration into existing platforms, and lower transaction costs, NFTs will become mainstream.

The simplification of the traditional finance system with the NFT increases the efficiency of the market. Here again, when an asset is digitally represented, it can eliminate the middlemen. It removes the tiring processes associated with traditional financial institutions, which in turn will make many workplaces redundant while creating new jobs for those who know how to use and implement NFTs.

We are seeing NFTs becoming a game-changer for digital art or collectibles. Until now, we are used to the easy copying process of digital files. We can duplicate digital files as often as we want, and every copy is exactly the same. Because of these properties of digital files, buying and collecting art and other digital items have never really made sense, making it extremely challenging to earn money as a digital artist or creator. In the art world, artists and content creators can use NFT technology to replicate certain characteristics that have so far been limited to items in the physical world: scarcity, uniqueness, and proof of ownership. Content creators can finally truly own and sell their digital work. This ability is creating a whole new market for original digital art and collectibles, attracting not only collectors but also new investors.

The digital tokens created essentially contain digital contracts outlining the rights of how the buyer and creator can use the work in the future. And there are other terms that creators can set as well, for example, granting certain commercial rights. The Bored Ape Yacht Club NFTs come with a license of commercial rights, for example, which opens up plenty of possibilities regarding how holders can monetize their tokens. Famous athletes have acquired Apes and sold-out multiple merchandise drops. You could also sell your license to an IP development company, such as Myth Division. They can then have a comic book with your Ape character created or a new soft drink "Ape Bull" that shows the Ape on the can or bottle label.

NFTs are also valuable because they can be minted from anything that can be digitized. The best way to look at NFTs is to see them as real-life collectors' objects, only that they are digital. So instead of investing in physical artwork or real estate, you get a digital copy that belongs to you until you sell it off. That way, you are the only owner of your NFT until you sell it. And since NFTs are on the blockchain—you guessed it—verifying their ownership and transferring it from one owner to another becomes a lot easier.

So far, we've talked about intangible, digital products linked to NFTs. But you can also set up NFTs for physical assets, making it attractive and convenient for owners to "own" a physical asset. They can own the NFT without ever having to take possession of the physical asset. This type of use of an NFT is likely to gain some momentum in the future because it makes trading physical assets easier and safer as long as it is professionally stored and insured against theft and damage.

The true advantage of NFTs is that they solve the problems of authenticity and provenance that are plaguing traditional art and collectibles, which you will discover in chapter 3 - History of NFTs. NFTs provide, of course, several advantages:

Authenticity

The fine art world requires experts to tell potential buyers whether a deceased artist has created a particular piece. However, with NFTs, the authenticity of each item is verified by the blockchain. As discussed, an NFT is a smart contract, and each smart contract has its own address. In the case of an Ethereum-based NFT, it would be a 42-character Ethereum address. Anyone can search in a block explorer for the NFT's address and find the NFT's smart contract. Additionally, the block explorer will show the address that originated the NFT. If the smart contract address matches the artist's address, the NFT is authentic. Otherwise, the NFT is not authentic and might be fake. No "experts" needed.

Proof of Ownership

NFTs are all about digital proof of ownership. Since NFTs have a transparent chain of title from the creator to the current owner on the blockchain, they have built-in provenance. As we described before, each transaction on the blockchain must be verified in the network. Each blockchain has its own block explorer website, on which you can do a search of an NFT's address or check the trading history on a marketplace. The block explorer website will show you the NFT's creator address, each successive owner, and the dates and amounts paid in cryptocurrency for each NFT transfer. These transactions are immutable once they're confirmed on the blockchain. For example, for the Ethereum blockchain, there's Etherscan (etherscan.io) and Ethplorer (ethplorer.io), and for Bitcoin, you can see all wallet transactions on btcscan.org or explorer.btc.com.

Today, when you need proof of ownership, you often need a piece of paper. When you buy a car or a house you will receive a piece of paper proving you are the owner. This proof of ownership will become paperless in the future using NFTs and blockchain technology. Concert tickets, conference tickets, and even flight tickets will become NFTs in the future.

Durability

Physical collectibles will degrade over time, and you have to invest money into their maintenance. NFTs on a blockchain provide permanence as long as the blockchain network is running. They cannot be accidentally damaged or destroyed. They can, theoretically, remain in pristine condition forever. However, the owner of an NFT can intentionally and permanently destroy it. This process is known as "burning" in the crypto scene.

Scarcity

It would be nice if you could copy the Bitcoin in your wallet so that you would have double the amount of Bitcoin, wouldn't it? Well, obviously, if this could be done, what would you think about the value of Bitcoin? If anyone could just copy it, Bitcoin would become meaningless. Just as you cannot copy a Bitcoin, you cannot copy NFTs. Usually, an NFT is a crypto token with a supply of one, which is documented on the blockchain. Non-fungible tokens opened up an entirely new market, which did not exist before, for digital artists and digital collectible creators. It has already generated millions for good reasons, and it will attract much more money in the future because creators are rewarded for every resell.

Retained Ownership for Creators

When a painter sells a painting, he or she will only be paid once. For every transaction on the secondary market to new collectors, the share is zero money for the creator. The painting could be sold 100 times for a price 10 times higher, but the creator will not benefit at all from the rising value of his or her work. NFTs can contain a continuing royalty, so creators can always participate in future sales of their work. And even better, the money will flow back automatically to the creator's crypto wallet. No invoice is necessary, nor waiting for the payment to be done. What a great way of generating passive income streams! For an artist, that's a revolutionary shift in how much control and compensation can be gained from a piece of creative work.

The downside is that currently ongoing royalties are guaranteed only if the NFT is sold on the same marketplace on which it was created. The payment might not work if the NFT is sold on a different marketplace.

To better understand why NFTs have value, let us also look at them from the aspect of collectibles. We'll do this because most NFTs are seen as digital collectibles, even if they have other uses. Collectibles are items with a limited supply that have value and are sought after by people known as collectors. Collectibles can range from very old and valuable items to new items produced in limited supplies. But why do people buy them?

Hobby or Passion

This is the main reason most people buy collectibles. Collecting is their hobby or passion, so they collect stamps, trading cards, or Legos for fun. The same goes for NFTs. Suppose you are a collector, and you decide to go digital. In that case, collecting NFTs is a way to fulfill that passion and feel the satisfaction that comes from collecting. And if you're only collecting NFTs, you don't need a spacious garage to store your trophies.

Investment

You can buy collectibles as an investment. Most collectors who buy these collectibles, especially art and ancient artifacts, know their value will increase. And if it does, they can resell them and make a profit.

Other investors can use collectibles as a store of value of assets. The physical art market declined dramatically during 2020–2021 because exhibitions were canceled due to Covid, so buyers and sellers could not gather together anymore. However, the big art dealers started to shift their focus to younger buyers and a generation of artists that is more present in the digital world and appreciates digital media. Therefore, it is likely that the digital art market will continue to grow.

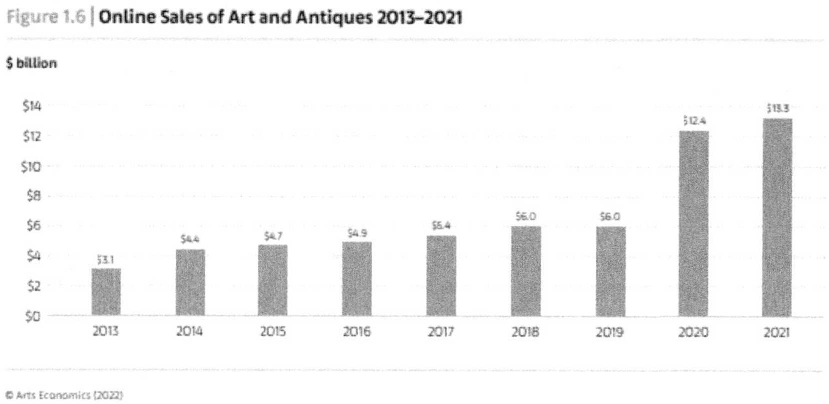

Image 7: Online sales volume of arts and antiques[19]

An art purchase worth $50,000 would still be worth $50,000 even after an economic crisis (provided it is not a fake). After 10 years, it can be worth a lot more. Like collectibles, NFTs can also help preserve their value during a downturn in the economy and help with inflation. Hence, more and more companies and institutions are acquiring them.

Unique Symbols for Social Status

Because collectibles have a limited supply, they are always difficult to get. This means that most people with highly valued collectibles are those with enough money or connections. The same also applies to NFTs. Take, for instance, Beeple's *Everydays*, worth 69 million dollars. Do you think it is owned by a working-class person? Even if they are broke, selling off that NFT or using it for collateral will land enough cash in their account to alter their social status.

Your Identity in a Metaverse

What is the metaverse, and why is it so important that Facebook changed its company name to Meta? The term "metaverse" originated in the 1992 dystopian novel "Snow Crash" by writer Neal Stephenson as an immersive digital environment where people interact as avatars.[20] It is a label for a digital or virtual world, also known as cyberspace. A metaverse can be accessed via virtual reality glasses or just via your Internet browser. It is important to understand that the metaverse is not one single digital world. There are different companies that are building their own metaverses and ecosystems in parallel.

A metaverse offers amazing possibilities. From shopping in a virtual world to traveling, going to virtual concerts, movies, collaborative work, and even testing new clothes or other fashion pieces, there are endless possibilities of what you can do with the metaverse in the future. This digital universe has proven to be more enterprising and innovative than we initially thought. It has expanded our frontier to a more interactive alternate reality with its decentralized economy. This alternate reality and the decentralized economy is the main link that connects NFTs to the metaverse.

NFTs in a metaverse can be anything from avatars, clothing, gaming items, virtual land, or pieces of digitized physical art. You can buy and sell NFTs in a metaverse with crypto tokens. Each metaverse often has its own currency token, for example, in the coming metaverse of the Bored Ape Yacht Club (called "The Otherside") there is an ApeCoin (APE), while in the metaverse "The Sandbox" the token Sand is being used.

NFTs have other functions in the metaverse aside from allowing us to access the metaverse or defining its future. Here are some of the NFT's other functions in the metaverse:

- NFTs help the metaverse to operate a transparent and fair economy. It allows people to represent their real-world assets in a digital environment that is decentralized, immutable, and transparent. The latter qualities are the function of the blockchain technology backing NFTs.
- NFTs will give individuals access to specific locations or lands in the metaverse. You can call it a property deed, only that it would be virtual. This has automatically transformed the design of digital and virtual interaction. These lands can be sold, developed, or even rented out.
- Using NFTs, enthusiasts with like minds can form virtual communities on the metaverse creating a whole new concept of identity.

You can download our Metaverse Investment Guide 2023 on our homepage **www.thevaluebird.com/bonus**

The Most Expensive NFT Projects

1. Pak's *Merge* - $91.8 million

Pak, the celebrated digital artist, created *The Merge*, which has become the most exorbitant NFT ever. The piece was fractionalized into 312,686 NFTs and sold to 28,983 buyers in December 2021 for $91.8 million on Nifty Gateway. The really amazing thing is that the opening price of each of these shares was $575, although it increased by $25 every six hours. Grossing over $91 million in sales, the NFT dislodged Jeff Moon's *Rabbit*. The 1986 painting sold for $91 million, but with *The Merge* totaling more than $91 million, Pak became the most valuable living artist ever.

2. Beeple's *Everydays* - $69.3 million

Have you ever imagined what drawing a digital image every day for more than a decade looks like? That's what Mike "Beeple" Winklemann, a digital artist, did. His work, a combination of 5,000 digital pieces he made consistently every day for upwards of thirteen years, made him a household name when sold. The NFT named *Everydays: The First 5000 Days* was bought by Vignesh Sundaresan, a crypto investor based in Singapore. Vignesh, also referred to as MetaKovan, founded the Metapurse NFT project. He bought the NFT at a Christie's art auction in 2021.[21]

Beeple's *Everydays* ranks as the second most expensive NFT ever sold. Generally, it is the fourth most expensive art from a living artist ever bought at an auction. Does the price surprise you? It may not when you discover that Beeple's other work also sold for high prices. Let's understand why this price was paid for his NFT.

Mike Winkelmann was a computer scientist who had no background in art. But he had the desire to draw, so he started to learn how to draw on a computer in his free time and he published his work every day. His followers could see his work and held him accountable for this. He wanted to create something and document his incremental improvement by starting every day again from zero to a completed image. In the first year, he produced mostly sketches and doodles, but he began learning Cinema 4D and mastering it day by day. He made the rule that he couldn't pre-plan or make templates to use if he was feeling lazy. He became famous by just doing what he loved. Because he established himself already as a leading native digital artist, the auction house Christie's approached Mike to do an NFT drop and convinced him to package the first 5,000 *Everydays* into one token. Here you can see the work on an IFPS storage:

https://ipfsgateway.makersplace.com/ipfs/QmXkxpwAHCtDXbbZHUwqt FucG1RMS6T87vi1CdvadfL7qA

He probably had no intention of selling his work for such a high price. But he did have his purpose, his "Why am I doing this every day?" He also aligned his brand to be an NFT artist. And he already sold digital art. It was not that he came from nowhere and sold tomorrow for $69.3 million. He had already sold his art for five figures and higher. He was authentic and gave to his community. He inspired others to develop a daily habit that helps them to master a certain work. Just as we (the publishers at Value Bird Publications) are learning about and trying to master the financial world every day. Buying a Beeple NFT gave each buyer and collector a kind of assurance that Beeple would continue to create a new piece each day into the future, which will of course grow his community and therefore the demand for his work.

On one hand, Christie's role in facilitating the sale of Beeple's work was seen as a powerful validation of NFTs by late adopters in the traditional art world. On the other hand, crypto purists criticized the whole process of this auction as being illegitimate and a betrayal of NFTs' true values. The revolutionary goal of NFTs is to eliminate gatekeepers and intermediaries of all types. Why pay a fee to insert a classic art-market middleman into an NFT sale, when NFTs were engineered in large part to eliminate dependence on middlemen? Instead of running the whole auction on MakersPlace, where all activity would be verified and archived on the blockchain, Christie's announced that the bidding for *Everydays* would instead take place via the same online interface the house uses for all their other auctions of artwork and collectibles. Where were the transparency and accountability if the competition for the token would all take place off-chain? Even if you reluctantly accepted Christie's presence and their marketing channels, how could their old-school process legitimize an actual NFT sale?[22]

Do you think the price was too high for this piece? The buyer, MetaKovan, is fractionalizing his collection via a B.20 token and is planning to create a digital art gallery that can be viewed in several metaverses. Now this image is the most famous one in the NFT world and it is drawing people's attention not because of its aesthetic, but because of its record sales price. If visitors in the metaverse are willing to pay just $1 to view the work, after a few years and maybe 69 million curious visitors, MetaKovan will start to make insane profits.

3. *Clock* from the Censored Collection - $52.7 million

The Clock is a symbolic NFT jointly created by Julian Assange and Pak. It shows the number of days Julian, the WikiLeaks founder, spent in jail in London.

Julian has been charged with espionage by the United States and is being held at the Belmarsh prison in London, awaiting extradition to the US. Following the model that was used to raise funds for Edward Snowden, the NSA whistleblower, *The Clock* was created to gather funds for Assange's defense, and in February 2022, it was auctioned for about $52.7 million dollars. This promptly made it the third most expensive NFT to ever be sold. *The Clock* NFT belongs to a large NFT collection named Censored. The Censored collection can be viewed in OpenSea and features more than 29,000 tokenized messages.

Beeple's *Human One* - $28.9 million

Beeple seems to have a talent for creating multi-million-dollar non-fungible tokens—and the *Human One* did not disappoint. The *Human One* is an animated video featuring an astronaut floating through various landscapes. The NFT was sold for $28.9 million at an auction in December 2021. Additionally, a smart contract embedded in the NFT allows Beeple to control what the video displays. In this way, *Human One* remains dynamic and progressive. Do you think it is worth the price?

CryptoPunk #5822 - $23.7 million

CryptoPunks have gathered much popularity because of their ever-recurring record-breaking sales. The CryptoPunks NFT projects began in 2017 by Larva Labs, and the inspiration for the project was the London punk community, cyberpunk groups, and electronic music stars like Daft Punk. CryptoPunk #5822 is the most expensive CryptoPunk and the fifth most expensive NFT overall. The NFT is a limited-edition work from the rarest Alien edition. The CEO of Chain, Deepak Thapliyal, coughed up a whopping $23.7 million to acquire the NFT.

CryptoPunk #7523 - $11.75 million

Scarcity drives value, and this is remarkably true of CryptoPunks. CryptoPunk #7523 is a rare commodity from the limited Alien CryptoPunks collection. There are just nine Alien Punks minted by Larva Labs. The CryptoPunk #7523 comes with special accessories ranging from earrings, medical masks, and a knitted cap.

So, the Alien CryptoPunk #7523 has good reason to be the second most expensive CryptoPunk out there. When Shalom Mackenzie, DraftKing's biggest shareholder, dished out almost $12 million to buy this NFT, they knew they were making a good investment.

CryptoPunk #4156 - $10.26 million

The CryptoPunk NFT series is clearly a huge industry. This sale was set in motion when a collector with the pseudonym Punk4156 felt that Larva Lab's communication, community engagement, and licensing guidance were less than desired and became dissatisfied with the whole NFT project. The NFT was bought for $10.26 million in 2021. Punk4156 is still in the NFT scene and is building an innovative project that builds open-source IP. This project is called Nouns.

CryptoPunk #5577 - $7.7 million

If you thought that the interest in CryptoPunks and trading of NFTs would be slow in 2022 because of the NFT frenzy that occurred in 2021, then you're mistaken. 2022 doesn't intend to slow down. As early as the first quarter of 2022, CryptoPunk #5577 sold for $7.7 million. The eccentric founder of Compound DeFi protocol, Robert Leshner, acquired the NFT and announced it on Twitter with a "Yeehaw."

CryptoPunk #3100 - $7.6 million

By now, you shouldn't be surprised to see another CryptoPunk on the list. It's no secret that investors have a soft spot for CryptoPunks, and

CryptoPunk #3100 is no different. Interestingly, it is among the limited Alien avatars. As you're well aware, the rarer the collection, the more valuable the art.

XCOPY's *Right-click and Save As guy* - $7,09 million

London-based artist XCOPY became a star in the NFT scene. Critics of NFT art are quick to point out that they can easily right-click and save the image of the artwork, without understanding that this has nothing to do with ownership. By now, you know that the fact that you can take a photo of a yacht or building doesn't turn you into the owner either. This particular animated work mocks those who do not believe in digital or crypto art and was sold for 1,600 ETH in December 2021.

How to Store Crypto and NFTs Safely

The understanding of different types of crypto wallets is essential when investing seriously in cryptocurrencies. In your NFT journey, you will come to a point where you need to decide where and how you will store your NFTs or crypto. Just as you need a bank account to store your fiat money, you would also need a so-called cryptocurrency wallet to store your cryptos and NFTs. There are different types of wallets. For each unique blockchain, you would need to have a different wallet with a different, unique wallet address. Most NFTs are using the Ethereum blockchain, even though other blockchains can be used for NFTs as well and they charge lower gas fees. For NFTs based on Ethereum, you would need a wallet that can hold tokens programmed for the ERC-20 standard—the Ethereum token standard as well as the ERC-721 and ERC-1155 standards for NFTs. If the NFTs are on a different blockchain such as WAX or FLOW you would need wallets that are made for those standards, but to keep it simple, we focus on Ethereum-compatible wallets.

MetaMask is currently the most popular Ethereum wallet for NFTs. We will explain how you create a MetaMask wallet in chapter 4.

It's important to be aware that technically you never store your cryptos and NFTs in your MetaMask or hardware wallet in the real sense of the word "store". They are always stored on a blockchain to a linked address. The wallet stores the keys, which you can access with your seed phrase. The seed phrase can be called the wallet since you will lose everything stored on that wallet if it's misplaced or lost. Everything! The wallet you use just filters out everything on the blockchain related to your address and gives you permission to transfer your assets. A MetaMask wallet is like a pair of foxy-orange glasses that you put on to see your assets on the Ethereum blockchain.

Knowing the best kind of wallets and the safest is your best shot at keeping your crypto and NFTs safe for a very long time. There are two types of blockchain wallets: hot wallets and cold wallets. If a wallet is connected to the Internet, it is a hot wallet, otherwise, if it is not connected to the Internet, it is a cold wallet. You can decide to keep your digital assets in either of the two types of wallets or in a combination of hot and cold.

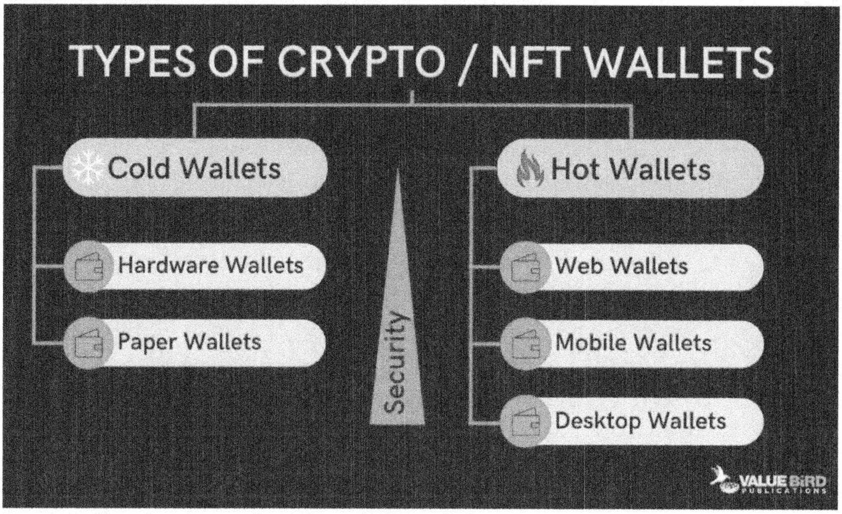

Image 8: Overview types of crypto and NFT wallets

Your choice of wallet will depend on a number of factors, which we'll discuss later. To keep things simple, let's start with cold wallets, the safer wallets, before talking about hot wallets.

Cold Wallets - The Safe Wallet

These wallets are offline, unlike hot wallets. They include hardware wallets and paper wallets. Cold wallets are the safest method of storing cryptos and NFTs. All your assets are stored offline and locked with a password.

Hardware Wallets

If you have to store your NFTs for a very long time, or you have very expensive NFTs, then you will need a trusted hardware wallet to secure your NFTs. Hardware wallets are usually special USB sticks you can purchase on the Internet. They offer the best security by completely avoiding the online exposure of your private keys because the private keys are saved on the physical device in an offline environment. Even if the device is connected to the Internet, the private key does not leave the device. The device would request the transaction details and provide validation for the data, thereby completing the transaction. The transaction details go to the online network to be stored on a blockchain.

Hardware wallets work just like flash drives and, of the cold wallets, are among the easiest-to-use crypto wallet because you can connect them at any time to computers by using a USB drive. Some of the popular hardware wallets that are in use presently include Trezor, Ledger, and many others from different manufacturers.

Another cool thing about these wallets is that they can also be used as hot wallets when needed. To do so, you would have to connect your wallet to an Internet source, which could simply be your mobile phone's Internet. Even when online, they are more secure than regular hot wallets. No need to worry about malicious attacks from viruses or hackers. Even if your computer is hacked, your wallet is safe because your NFTs' information is not on the device but rather in your hardware wallet. However, just because a wallet is a hardware wallet doesn't mean that it is automatically safe. When buying NFT wallets, be mindful of which wallets you get. Never buy a second-hand hardware wallet or even a new one from marketplaces such as eBay or Amazon because the seller might have manipulated the wallet you buy. They could potentially pull out your hard-earned cryptos years later. It is best to buy your wallet directly from a company's official website to avoid buying an already compromised wallet. The best hardware wallet is Ledger, but other types that are safe for your NFTs are Trezor, BitBox, and Ngrave.

Paper Wallets

Paper wallets are cold wallets and nothing but physical pieces of paper. The paper must contain all the data you would need for accessing your cryptocurrency, which is a pair of private and public keys that you need to use in transactions. They are created using key generator programs and then printed on a sheet of paper. They consist of two-character strings and quick response codes (QR Codes).

Paper wallets are, of course, not connected to the Internet. It was once upon a time one of the best ways of storing cryptos or other digital assets. Their disadvantages are their more time-consuming handling and in the event of losing the paper document, the risk of losing the crypto assets in the wallet.

Hot Wallets - The Convenient Wallet

Hot wallets are basically software wallets that connect to the Internet, which results in less security because they are more vulnerable to online attacks. If so, why do people still use them? They use them because hot wallets offer better accessibility due to their connection to the Internet. Although less secure, hot wallets are very easy to use, making spending and trading cryptos or NFTs much easier. Even if hot wallets are vulnerable to fraudsters and hacker attacks, they are highly user-friendly. For example, it would be rather inconvenient to trade or buy something with cryptocurrency in your cold than in a mobile hot wallet. You would need to find a computer in which to plug your USB cold wallet, then move the required amount of cryptocurrency to a hot wallet, and then make your purchase.

Nevertheless, we do not recommend holding large amounts of cryptocurrency or valuable NFTs in a hot wallet. If you have a significant amount in a hot wallet, transfer it to a cold wallet to keep it safe. Professional crypto investors leave the bulk of their crypto assets in cold wallets and allow some small amounts for trading in a hot wallet for easy withdrawals or directly on a crypto exchange wallet. Cryptocurrency exchanges generally offer hot storage methods for their users. Their wallets are custodial because they hold your keys for you.

There are several types of hot wallets, and the most common ones include:

- Web-based wallets (= a website where you log in)
- Mobile wallets (= an app on tablets or phones, both android and iOS)
- Desktop wallets (= software or a browser extension on your desktop or laptop computer)

Web Wallets

Of the three kinds of hot wallets, a web-based wallet is the least safe but the most convenient. You can access the web wallets through a web browser without the need for downloading any specialized software or application. Because this wallet is Internet browser-based, you can access your crypto assets with your password from any location and any device as long as you can open a web browser. However, most of these web wallets would have ownership of the private keys to your crypto assets, which is a major negative point.

Mobile Wallets

The great advantage of mobile wallets is that they are portable, and you can access them even while sitting on, say, a train. Being portable, however, is also their greatest disadvantage, because you can easily forget your phone somewhere or worse, have it stolen. And then there are also cloud backups of your apps, so you never know who can see your data. There is always a solution, however, when there is a problem, although it isn't 100% effective. Instead of using your mobile wallet on your main smartphone, you can buy a second, cheap smartphone that you never carry with you but instead leave at home. You only turn it on when you want to transfer or make transactions with your assets. If you intend to use this hot wallet, research the wallets, and ensure they are safe for you. Do a great amount of research before you install a mobile wallet and make sure you installed it from a trusted source. Be aware that there are also fake apps in those official app stores that have the intention of stealing your cryptos. Google and Apple do not look in detail at every app that is being registered with their stores. Popular mobile wallet options include Coinbase Wallet (a separate app from the Coinbase crypto exchange), Mycelium, and Trust Wallet (a separate app from the Binance crypto exchange).

Desktop Wallets

Desktop wallets are safer than mobile and web-based wallets but are not as safe as hardware or cold wallets. There are wallets for Windows desktops, Mac OS, and Linux that you can install locally on your computer. After installing, you will receive your private keys and you should also create a secure password to access the wallet software. The main benefits of desktop wallets are that you are in charge of your private keys, like in mobile wallets. There is no need for an intermediary.

Popular desktop wallets are MetaMask, Atomic Wallet, and Exodus. There are often mobile wallet versions of desktop wallets.

Summary

An understanding of different types of crypto wallets is quite essential for investments in cryptocurrencies. As you can see, each of these types of crypto wallets has advantages and disadvantages. You need to decide which storage option for your cryptocurrencies offers you the right balance of functionality and security. We believe it is optimal to use a combination of a cold wallet to store your long-term holdings and a hot wallet to store the smaller amounts you use for crypto trading or payments.

Where Is the NFT Content Stored?

Now that we understand where to store our NFTs and cryptocurrencies, it is now crucial to understand where the NFT content—meaning the images, music, videos, 3D models, etc.—is being stored.

As long as the blockchain exists, you permanently own that NFT you like so much (unless you decide to sell it, of course). The blockchain also confirms that the artists you bought it from actually created it. But where is the content file stored, and is it a safe place?

Most content (videos, music, or image files) of NFTs don't really permanently live on a blockchain. It would take too much storage capacity to store the large image and video files on the blockchain. Therefore, only the NFT's metadata is stored on the blockchain with a reference to the digital file, which is stored separately from the smart contract itself.

To store content files off-chain there are two main solutions available:

1. The first solution is a cloud storage solution. This could be Amazon AWS, Google Cloud, Hewlett Packard (HP) Cloud, Microsoft Azure, Salesforce Cloud, Snowflake, and many more.
2. The second solution is the InterPlanetary File System (IPFS). The IPFS is a decentralized peer-to-peer network of computers around the world where data is stored across several locations. As long as the network continues to be supported, the content is usually safe.

Although these are the two main solutions, the content files can pretty much be stored anywhere on the Internet. An NFT is technically just a reference to a digital asset, and we recommend keeping a copy of the files in another safe drive. Why? Because these digital assets can be erased, and sometimes even the server that hosts it could be hacked, fail, or be switched off without any notice. If this happens, the NFT might become worthless or drastically reduce its value. Currently, there is no law to address this situation, but if you have a copy in another place, you would still be the owner and might have certain license rights. Therefore, the responsibility falls to you to ensure your NFTs are secured after buying them.

Don't just buy your NFTs and think they are safe. You need to take precautionary measures, too. The content storage problem of NFTs is actually a very serious one. Did you hear about what happened to the NFT album of musician 3LAU that sold on Nifty Gateway for $11 million? After the sale, it went missing. It existed only on a centralized provider, a business that could eventually go bust, as so many businesses eventually do.[23]

NFT marketplaces such as OpenSea pay for storage, but what happens to your NFT content when the marketplace goes offline because it is bankrupt and cannot pay the cloud server cost anymore? Creators can also store the NFT content on a private server that permanently shuts down. These ugly scenarios are in harsh contrast to all the great benefits NFTs have, such as providing a trustless peer-to-peer transaction. Also, for the unlockable content, the storage is usually only a link to more images, music, or videos, which are somewhere hosted on the Internet. What happens if the content creator no longer maintains the website or server? We recommend backing up the original files, so you have a copy of it just in case the external link disappears. The second storing solution we mentioned might save the problem for good:

InterPlanetary File System (IPFS)

InterPlanetary File Systems, also known as IPFS, can be used for the off-chain storage of your NFTs. This reduces the risk of your content being deleted or removed. Why? The IPFS enables users to download a file from many locations that aren't managed by one organization. If the content file is stored only on one central server and this server is being attacked or the server catches fire, your content would be lost. It also makes it harder to censor content because it is stored in many places. It will also try to retrieve your file from some server nearby instead of a central location far away, which could speed up your download. It could also help within one larger organization, such as a corporation or research center, to retrieve information quickly without going to the worldwide Internet and risking downloading a malicious source code.

A traditional file path would give an exact location of *where* a file is stored on a computer or website and typically look like:

- https://www.thevaluebird.com/download/nft-checklist.pdf
- \Users\Carmen\Desktop\white_paper.doc
- C:\Users\John\My Documents\nft_presentation.ppt

The IPFS would not specify *where* a file is located but use instead a content identifier that specifies *what* the content is, and it would be identical in the different stored location. The IPFS content identifier (CID) is a long cryptic, alphanumeric string—a so-called "hash"—which is unique for each piece of content. The IPFS content identifier could point to a single file (no matter what file size), a complete file directory, or a whole website. The problem with this method is only that the link can't be changed. Every new version of the content needs a new CID, and the content can't be moved to a different address. But this is exactly what you want when acquiring an NFT.[24]

Users who participate in the file storage network ensuring data continues to exist are rewarded with an alternative crypto coin called Filecoin (FIL).[25]

Gas Fees

When we talk about gas fees with respect to NFTs, we're not talking about the price you pay at the petrol station when you fill up your vehicle (Thank goodness right? No one wants to pay more of *those*). We're talking about transaction fees on a blockchain network, which is known as gas fees, or simply gas. Gas fees have risen tremendously for Ethereum in recent years and have gotten out of control reaching at rush hours up to a ridiculous $800 for one transaction. Since the change of Ethereum from proof of work to proof of stake mechanism in September 2022, they are much lower, but still high compared to other cryptocurrencies or tokens such as Polygon. Gas fees go to the miners (validators) who process transactions on the blockchain network. The amount of gas required for a certain transaction is based on two main factors.

1. First, they are based on the type of transaction and its required computational power to execute the operation. A simple transfer of ETH or an NFT from one wallet to another will require lower gas fees. If you're deploying a lengthy smart contract to the network, the gas fee will be significantly higher.

2. The second factor affecting the gas fee is the current transaction volume. The higher the volume, the more demand is created, which drives up the price of gas. High transaction volume is also called "congestion." If you have ever used Uber to call a car, you will know that during busy rush hours the prices increase.

Ethereum was not originally built for such a high transaction volume, and since it became the second most important cryptocurrency after Bitcoin, the volume increased beyond the expectations of its developers. However, the team behind Ethereum is aware of this problem and has promised future updates which will hopefully solve these painful gas fees.

But keep in mind that Ethereum is not the only blockchain that is suitable for NFTs. All the other ones competing with Ethereum have significantly lower transaction fees, which is why they are becoming more and more popular. These alternative blockchains are using the easier proof of stake method to validate blocks instead of the proof of work method, which Bitcoin is using. Speaking of Bitcoin, it also has rather high transaction fees.

Now that you know about the different types of NFTs, their value, benefits, and how to store them. What next? Well, how to buy one of course! But hold for just a bit, because we're going to use the next chapter to discuss the history of NFTs before diving into the rest.

Chapter 3: The History of NFTs

Problems with Traditional Art and Collectibles

In the fine art world, the authenticity of a piece is essential to its value. Whether it's an original or not can make a difference of several million dollars. One of the biggest problems in the traditional art world is that forgeries and fakes have been smuggled into the art market for hundreds of years.

Switzerland's Fine Art Expert Institute (FAEI) has issued warnings for collectors across the art market: they estimate that 50 percent of circulating art on the market is being forged or misattributed.[26] We assume this figure is too high and just a clever marketing announcement—this institute charges up to $19,000 to verify a painting. Even though they are basically living off the fear of art collectors, it indicates that the traditional art market also attracts many swindlers. But surely you are looking at an original painting in museums, galleries, private collections, and auctions? Ladies and gentlemen, we would like to bring to your attention some quite astonishing high-profile art scams in recent history:

Dutch artist Han van Meegeren (1889 - 1947) developed a complicated system of baking his "old masters" to age them and subsequently sold fake Vermeers for a total of $60 million to world-class museums in the 1930s and 1940s.[27]

The Knoedler Forgery Ring had to close in 2011 after the forgeries—that they sold for $80 million—were discovered. They sold more than 20 fakes of Jackson Pollock, Mark Rothko, Robert Motherwell, and other artists via their venerable Knoedler gallery. The ringleaders also created forged provenance documents.

A $250 million heist in Turkey happened in the State Art and Sculpture Museum in Ankara, where museum officials teamed up with criminals to steal more than 300 works from the museum between 2005 and 2009. At some stage, the museum realized that 46 pieces in the collection had been replaced by copies.

The Beltracchis in Freiburg, Germany sold false works of Max Ernst and Heinrich Campendonk for a minimum of $22 million to several collectors via Sotheby's and Christie's auctions, and even one forgery to the Metropolitan Museum of Art in New York City.[28]

British art restorer (and forger) Tom Keating confessed to having faked over 2,000 paintings by more than 100 different artists, including Rembrandt and Samuel Palmer. His counterfeits are still selling on the market between for £5,000 and £10,000.[29]

The list continues, we think you get the idea. And the problem of forgeries not only applies to physical art, but also to collectible items.

In the fine art world, authenticity is being assessed by so-called connoisseurs. These experts will look at the type of canvas and the stretchers used, the paints and material, and its documentation. Eventually, the connoisseur will authenticate the work. However, there are no standards for what the connoisseur does, no licensing, and no credentials other than experience. The accuracy of the connoisseurship examination depends on the knowledge, experience, and skills and is therefore highly subjective. [30]

The high-end art world is also like a social club. If they don't want you to join, you will have a difficult life as an artist. In the 2006 documentary *Who the #$&% Is Jackson Pollock?* a 73-year-old former truck driver bought a painting from a thrift shop for $5 and found out later it could be a Jackson Pollock painting. Not only does this documentary expose social class barriers, but also how difficult it can be for outsiders of the fine art world to receive recognition. Since the painting the former truck driver bought was lacking provenance, the experts rejected it as an original, claiming it was too "neat" and therefore can't be a Jackson Pollock.

The former truck driver nevertheless hired a forensic scientist who found a fingerprint on the back of the painting that matched with a fingerprint from a paint can at Pollock's workshop, which would change the value to $50 million and more. Yet the snobby "art experts" refused to accept it as an original Pollock, while many forgeries authenticated by art connoisseurs continue to be hanging in galleries and museums.[31] [32]

The rejection of the painting has less to do with the artwork itself than with the person who found it. "Here I am, a former truck driver. I'm 75 with an eighth-grade education. I don't fit into the elite New York art world. If a lady of name had found this painting, it would have been sold a long time ago. But they don't want to listen to me. I've heard from people around the world who have Picassos and Turners and they can't get them into the art houses, and it's only because of who they are."[33]

Authentic documentation leading back to the artist would have solved the problem. Often, newly discovered artwork has no provenance documentation or sometimes has fake documents. Fraudsters were even caught inserting fake provenance documents into the archives of the Tate Gallery and others to sell their high-priced forgeries.[34]

We hope you can see now how NFTs can solve a big problem in the art world. But not just there. We expect in the future our lives will be full of NFTs. How can we trust any art currently if the artist has passed away?

And when it comes to collectibles, the estimated size of the global market in 2020 was $370 billion.[35]

And it is estimated to grow to $522 billion by 2028.

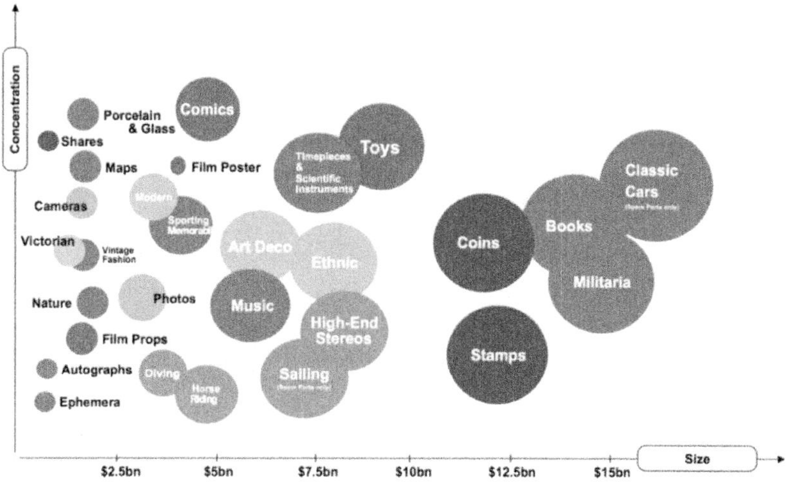

Image 9: Collectible Segment Map[36]

Similar to the art world, as the value of certain items can be quite high, it naturally attracts fraudsters and forgeries. A large percentage of what is being sold online is either looted or fake. In the 1990s, the FBI started a large sport and celebrity memorabilia market investigation called Operation Bullpen. They dismantled 18 forgery rings and arrested 63 individuals who were involved in faking signatures. Memorabilia experts estimate forged memorabilia comprises over $100 million of the market each year—time to introduce blockchain technology here, too, don't you think?[37]

The First Digital Art (Before NFTs)

Digital art is art that only exists in a digital medium. It is rather a new form of art, which started in the 1950s. Artists were working with mechanical devices and analog computers. They often had to program the computers themselves, since there was no user interface, and the mouse was invented later. Output devices were also limited. In the 1960s, plotters were available, a mechanical device linked to a computer to control the movements of a pen that it holds. The drawings were mostly linear due to their technical structure.

When computers became a mass consumer product in the late 1980s, the medium gained in popularity. Artists started to use computers (and later smartphones and tablets) as a tool to create art in a new medium type. Computer graphics entered TV and film such as in *Star Trek*, and computer games began to crawl into families' homes.

And yet computer art was not respected in the fine art world. Perhaps because computers were[38] seen as machines that only process zeros and ones. Or perhaps people felt that the artist's soul was missing in digital art? Can digital art truly express the inner emotions of an artist? Or perhaps because computer programmers were mostly nerds, engineers who were not understood by eccentric artists. Not being allowed into fine art society, computer engineers built their own community instead.

In 1968, the Computer Arts Society was founded to promote the creative uses of computers in arts and culture: www.computer-arts-society.com.

A shift happened in 1984 when Steve Jobs introduced the Macintosh computer, which came with a graphical user interface allowing the average person to interact with computers. Anyone who purchased MacPaint software had the ability to create their own digital art. A few years later, Adobe's Photoshop software and Corel Draw and Corel Painter followed. Because new software made it easier and easier for artists to create their work, the community of digital art grew. In 1992, Wacom launched the first tablet with a cordless stylus that gave artists even more freedom and flexibility to work.

As large record labels painfully discovered, digital files can be copied and shared on the Internet in seconds. There won't be any loss of quality, only the album cover or booklet would be missing. The music industry tried to develop digital rights management (DRM), but we users personally had a very bad experience with this. Copying mp3 files we officially paid for on other devices was possible, but they just wouldn't play and show a DRM error message instead. We bought the mp3 music from a hip marketplace called MusicLoad which went offline after a year or so, so we couldn't ask anyone for support anymore.

Now, streaming services such as Amazon Music, Apple Music, Spotify, or Tidal are widely used but pay very little to artists.

Since the year 2000, digital art museums popped up all over the world contributing to the growth in that market.

The first NFT was probably created by Kevin McCoy, a professor at New York University and a digital artist. He minted his non-fungible token, *Quantum*, on May 3rd, 2014—years before the crypto art market exploded. *Quantum* is a pixelated, animated gif of an octagon in fluorescent hues that changes shapes, hypnotically pulsing. The *Quantum* art is on sale for $7 million dollars.

In the year 2014, Ethereum did not yet exist. In 2014, Vitalik Buterin and the other co-founders of Ethereum raised more than $18 million from a crowdsourcing campaign where they sold participants Ethereum tokens to get their vision off the ground. Buterin was looking for a solution for all use cases for blockchains and wanted to overcome the limitations of Bitcoin.[39]

The first blockchain game was launched in 2015, called Spells of Genesis. The game's creators focused fully on in-game assets and also created their own in-game currency.

In 2017 CryptoPunks, a collection of 10,000 pixelated profile images, was launched by Larva Labs creators John Watkinson and Matt Hall. CryptoPunks cemented the NFT trend and paved the way for the storm that came a few years after. In the same year, CryptoKitties was created by Dapper Labs and MoonCats by Ponderware, which exploded in fame and price as well. Choosing cats for a collectible was a wise decision—the Internet has a huge cat fan community (Grumpy Cat, anyone?). For years, there has been a satirical website online featuring photographs of cats resembling Adolf Hitler (www.catsthatlooklikehitler.com) and of course, there are thousands of Instagram profiles and YouTube channels dedicated to cat content. It is astonishing how many people enjoy going on YouTube to watch funny cat videos. Therefore, CryptoKitties also helped to reach a critical mass for collecting NFTs, especially since owners of two CryptoKitties can breed a new cat that is the genetic combination of its parents. The CryptoKitties game became an instant hit. Because of the huge following CryptoKitties generated, Dapper Labs received $12 million from Venture Capitalist Union Square. They also changed from the Ethereum to the Flow blockchain because they caused congestion on Ethereum in December 2017[40].

We believe digital art was not the only factor that led to the creation of NFTs. There were also other art movements that would influence the taste of art collectors. However, all the headline-grabbing selling prices for NFTs would not be possible without the long history of artists who tried to break the barriers of what is considered art.

The Pop Art Movement

Andy Warhol started first to sell commercial art—illustrations for magazines and advertisements. But he was ambitious enough not to stay a commercial illustrator and graphic designer. He wanted to get famous in the fine art world as well. As we know already, not everyone gets into this club.

He started with exhibitions in California but did not sell very much. But he did contribute to a new, Pop Art movement. By creating artwork of mass culture objects, comic books, and media stars, the Pop Art movement aimed to blur the boundaries between "high" art and "low" culture. Andy Warhol knew that Pop Art was the first art movement accessible to the average person and therefore continues to reflect the new consumerism movement showing them in a new light.

Andy tried to surround himself with artists and celebrities, which helped him to achieve living icon status. One intention of his works was to expand our awareness of images that everyone encounters daily but don't actually perceive as art: street posters, billboards, magazines, product labels, photos, and celebrities.

Roy Lichtenstein, Robert Rauschenberg, and James Rosenquist were growing with the Pop Art movement as well, but Andy Warhol was probably the most influential artist. He did not create it himself, but helped to change the perception of art worldwide: For centuries, people regarded "art" only as specific paintings, sculptures, music, and literature. With Pop Art, the consideration and appreciation of what is "art" became more diverse. Without the Pop Art movement, there wouldn't be as many art collectors existing at all levels of society as we have today. Our imagination of what is artwork has expanded so drastically that even street graffiti (Banksy), an unmade, filthy bed (Tracey Emin), or a shark preserved in formaldehyde sell as art for millions.

Andy was the first artist to use the Amiga personal computer introduced in 1984 to digitally generate new art forms.[41]

Andy used the new computer software ProPaint in front of a live audience to create a portrait of Debbie Harry. He later made a series of digital drawings including a Campbell's soup can, Botticelli's *The Birth of Venus*, and flowers.[42]

While Andy Warhol was the figurehead of Pop Art, Beeple is the figurehead of the NFT art movement. Mike Winkelmann's continued work broke the barrier for digital-native artists all over the world who will now receive now more attention and respect thanks to his sale of *Everydays-The First 5000 Days*. For many years, digital artists have been given the impression their work is not "real art." But, luckily for everyone, the world's perception of art is changing.

Chapter 4: Buy Your First NFT In 5 Easy Steps

If you have reached this part of the book, we can comfortably say you have discovered all there is to know about NFTs and are ready for the real deal—buying an NFT. But remember that before buying an NFT, you must do some homework. Which type of NFT are you interested in the most?

Once you see an NFT you like, have researched the creator, the community, and the project itself, and have decided to use the money, you are ready to buy your first NFT. Isn't it exciting? And buying is even easier than you may think.

Before we begin, the process of buying NFTs is not definite. It can vary, but they are always almost the same. But sticking to the steps we'll outline below will help you avoid some risks in a scam-infested NFT world.

In order to buy NFTs, you need some prerequisites. If you were to go and invest in the stock market today, the first thing you would need is a trading account. Without a trading account in which you can hold your stocks, you cannot buy or sell any shares. Our trading account for NFTs is a digital wallet, and the stockbroker will be an NFT marketplace such as OpenSea.

Step 1: Create Your Own Wallet

The first step to buying your first NFT is to open a wallet for the cryptocurrencies you will need for that purchase and for future NFTS. **For security reasons, we highly recommend using a desktop computer for creating your wallet instead of your smartphone.** We also recommend not using wallets on a crypto exchange, but a wallet that can operate independently, giving you full control of your keys and your wallet, where you store your NFTs.

So which wallets are you going for? Hot wallets or cold wallets? Hot wallets are easy to use and more convenient. But they are also very prone to thefts and hacks. On the other hand, a cold wallet is more secure, although your risk of losing your entire assets is high since there is no backup in case of a lost phrase.

To start with, go for an Ethereum-compatible wallet since Ethereum is the blockchain where most NFTs are created and sold. Currently, the MetaMask wallet is a very popular wallet in the NFT scene because you can easily link it with OpenSea and other NFT marketplaces via a simple, free extension to your browser (Chrome, Firefox, or Brave). Instead of logging in with a user or email address and password, you just use the MetaMask browser extension.

When you click on the profile button top right on OpenSea you will also see what alternative wallets OpenSea supports. But in the following, we will guide you through the process of creating a MetaMask wallet.

We also offer an online course on our website www.thevaluebird.com in which we'll walk you through, step-by-step, how to buy your first NFT. In our video tutorials, we show in detail where to click and what to do. Here in this book, we will describe the simplified steps:

- Open your Chrome, Firefox, or Brave browser on your computer
- Search in the settings for the extension menu. Most browsers have their own extension stores. In the extension store search for "MetaMask" which has the logo of an orange fox. Click on "Install" or "Add" to install it.
- Find the extension icon (usually in the upper right corner of your browser) and click on the MetaMask fox to create a new account.

- Create a new wallet by choosing the right option "Create a wallet." You can use the left option "Import Wallet" on another computer where you enter the 12-word seed phrase and make a duplicate wallet.
- Then, you will be asked to create a password for your account. This password has nothing to do with the private key of your wallet. You need to keep this password secure as well, but it is only to access the MetaMask wallet extension in your browser. It is best to create strong passwords that other people can't easily guess, such as your birthday. A secure password should contain numbers, upper- and lower-case letters, and special characters such as #+%$§!? arranged uniquely.
- Proceed until you come to the page "Click Reveal Secret Words." There you will see your 12-word seed phrase. These words and their sequence are really important. Do not store them digitally on your computer or on your smartphone, so take your time and write them down. Do not lose the paper and keep it in a safe place.
- In the next step, you can verify the seed phrase. Once you have confirmed it, congrats, your wallet is ready to go. You can copy your public wallet address at the top of the MetaMask screen.

Please note that it is very easy to create multiple wallets in your MetaMask extension and you can give each wallet a specific name for its purpose. Why have multiple wallets? It makes sense that you keep separate wallets for each marketplace, so you do not confuse from where you bought which NFTs. Also for minting, we recommend using a separate wallet in which you only load the little amount of Ethereum that is required for minting. After minting, you send the NFT to a different wallet for storing it safely (on a Ledger or Trezor hardware wallet, for example). To create a new MetaMask wallet, simply click the circular button in the upper right of the extension and then click "Create Account." Once finished you can easily toggle between your wallets by clicking the same circular button again.

Now you need to fill your wallet with some crypto money, which you can use in step 5 to purchase your first NFT.

Step 2: Buy Ethereum

After opening a wallet, you'll need to buy crypto. This is because in most NFT marketplaces, you cannot pay in dollars or other fiat currencies. Therefore, our second step to buying your first NFT is to buy Ethereum (ETH), the native crypto that powers the Ethereum blockchain. Why? Because most of the NFTs are built on this blockchain. For some NFTs, you need other Cryptocurrencies like WAX, Solana (SOL), Flow (FLOW) or Polygon (MATIC), which are faster and have lower transaction fees than Ethereum. But to keep things easy, we'll start with the market leader ETH.

In your MetaMask wallet, you can only store cryptocurrencies of the ERC-20 standard because MetaMask is an Ethereum-based wallet. You can send Ethereum (ETH) or Tether (USDT) to that wallet address, but never send Bitcoins to that wallet address because you will lose them. Bitcoin does not use the ERC-20 standard, so they will disappear into the crypto nirvana. Since Ethereum (ETH) is the most popular blockchain for NFTs, let's get some together!

To exchange some fiat currency for Ethereum, you will need to open an account on an exchange. Exchanges work as brokerages and allow you to buy cryptocurrencies and sell them. No exchange is 100 % secure, so you should never keep a large amount of cryptocurrency in an exchange. You have a wallet in the exchange, but you don't have the private key to your wallet, which means if the exchange closes overnight, you might never see your money again.

We will recommend some exchanges that we believe are currently the best exchanges for buying and selling Ethereum, Polygon, Solana, and other cryptocurrencies. But always do your own research and pick the one you trust the most. Also, take into consideration that every exchange has different transaction fees and not all cryptocurrencies are available on every exchange. But you can always buy Ethereum and Bitcoin because they are the most relevant blockchains.

> *Warning: In the US, your money in bank accounts is insured up to $250,000 by the FDIC—the Federal Deposit Insurance Corp. The FDIC is an independent US agency that insures deposits and helps protect customers in case of given bank failures and has made it officially clear that cryptos aren't FDIC-insured. Therefore, users of cryptocurrency exchanges could potentially lose their funds!*[43]

Best Crypto Exchanges for Buying and Selling Ethereum

These are the most established exchanges (we use them ourselves). They have been on the market for years and have implemented high security levels. You can also check their ranking and stats here www.coingecko.com/en/exchanges:

Top Crypto Exchanges Ranked by Trust Score

As of today, we track 494 crypto exchanges with a total 24h trading volume of $72.7 Billion, a -3.32% change in the last 24 hours. Currently, the 3 largest cryptocurrency exchanges are Binance, Coinbase Exchange, and OKX.

All Countries — Overview | Cybersecurity New | Social

#	Exchange	Trust Score	24h Volume (Normalized)	24h Volume	Visits (SimilarWeb)	# Coins	# Pairs	Last 7 Days
1	Binance	10	$11,714,494,982	$11,714,494,982	87,122,346.0	356	1458	
2	Coinbase Exchange	10	$1,528,186,162	$1,528,186,162	6,213,662.0	212	525	
3	OKX	10	$1,345,745,097	$1,345,745,097	7,237,175.0	344	618	

Image 10: Crypto Exchanges Rank by Coingecko

Binance	www.binance.com

This is one of, if not the largest and biggest crypto exchange and trading platform. This exchange offers over 600 cryptocurrencies and charges about 0.1% for trading. It also offers NFTs and allows users to stake their crypto. It is one of the exchanges that is easiest to use.
If you live in the US, you have to use www.binance.us where only < 100 coins are available.

Pros

- largest trade volume of all exchanges
- low fees
- > 300 coins
- NFT marketplace
- earn dividends from staking coins
- you buy coins via credit card or bank transfer

Cons

- short trading is not possible in all countries
- has been hacked some years ago
- user interface may be too complicated for beginners
- not available for US users

Coinbase	www.coinbase.com

Based in the USA and the US stock exchange, Coinbase is the exchange with the second largest trading volume after Binance. Because this company is listed on a stock exchange, it has to follow certain regulations and transparency rules. It reported a net loss of $1.1 billion in the second quarter of 2022, a record for the company, and it had to cut its workforce by 18% in June of that same year[44]. But in August 2022, they announced a partnership with BlockRock, the world's largest asset manager. What concerns us about Coinbase is that they even warn their users that they could lose their crypto holdings on the platform if the company goes bankrupt. Users' crypto assets could become company property if it goes bankrupt. If you hold stocks on a broker account, you will still own the stocks even if the broker goes bankrupt. This is not the case with cryptocurrencies.[45] For this reason, we do not recommend keeping large amounts of coins on any of these exchanges. For long-term holdings, please always transfer them to a hardware wallet. You can find more information on this in our cryptocurrency handbook.

Pros	Cons
• easy user interface, best for amateur crypto enthusiasts • NFT marketplace • lots of educational resources	• high fees • limited choice of coins (> 200) • limited staking opportunities • short trading is not possible

OKX — www.okx.com

Based in Seychelles, this platform has high trading volume and offers various trading instruments. The former name was OKEx. For beginners, it might be too complex.
If you live in the US, you have to use OKCoin, where fewer coins and features are available.

Pros

- good choice of coins (> 300)
- short trading possible
- option trading possible (advanced traders)
- earn dividends from staking coins
- buy coins with credit card
- multilingual in 20 languages

Cons

- user interface may be too complex for beginners
- complex fee structure
- not available for US users

KuCoin — www.kucoin.com

Based in Seychelles as well it has grown to a popular exchange with high trading volume and millions of users. It was subject to a major hack in 2020, but the stolen cryptos were covered by insurance funds. If you live in the US, you can register, but you risk US regulators blocking your account for withdrawals.

Pros

- best choice of coins (> 700)
- low trading fees
- short trading possible
- earn dividends from staking coins
- buy coins with credit card
- multilingual in 20 languages

Cons

- user interface may be too complex for beginners
- not available for US users
- withdrawal fees charges

Step 3: Transfer Ethereum to Your Crypto Wallet

After you have acquired some Ethereum, you need to transfer some to your MetaMask wallet. Be very careful with every transfer of cryptocurrencies. Your money can easily disappear when you make a mistake. To avoid sending your precious cryptos to the wrong wallet address, always copy and paste (never type manually) your address and check the first and the last digits twice to make sure you copied the right address (unless you want to give a nice gift to a random person). Also, make sure the sending and receiving wallets support the ERC-20 standard. You can also send ETH on a polygon or other blockchain, which costs lower gas fees, but then you will have trouble seeing it in your MetaMask wallet. We always recommend trying a small amount first if you have a new wallet or are using a new platform. Transfer the minimum allowed ($5-10, depending on the platform you send it from) and see if the amount arrives in your MetaMask wallet. Be patient, sometimes it can take up to 30 minutes to arrive when the network is congested, but usually, it is faster. Once you see your transferred amount in your MetaMask wallet you are ready to buy your first NFT. Nice!

Never transfer all your Ethereum into your MetaMask wallet, only transfer the amount you need to buy your NFTs plus a bit more for gas fees. Please note that the gas fees are usually not fixed. As mentioned before, the amount of gas charged for each transaction depends on how complex it is and how congested the network is.

Step 4: Connect Your Wallet to the Marketplace

After filling your MetaMask wallet with ETH crypto, it's time to start the actual buying. But you can't do that if you don't link your wallet to the marketplace where you'll get your NFTs. On NFT marketplaces like OpenSea, your account is not linked to your email address, but to your wallet address. You don't need an email anymore to buy and sell. So let's go to www.opensea.io and get your first NFT.

On the top right you will see a wallet button on their homepage. If you click the wallet symbol you will be shown different wallet options, so look for the orange fox and "MetaMask" and click there. Now your browser extension should open automatically, and you need to enter the password that you used for your MetaMask wallet. Then you are connected, and you can start looking for an NFT you like.

Step 5: Buy Your First NFT

While browsing on OpenSea, you might notice the cryptocurrency WETH. What is WETH? It is a token with the same value as Ethereum, but it is called Wrapped Ethereum. You can easily swap ETH for WETH on OpenSea. The benefit of using WETH instead of ETH is that it comes with more functionality for making offers on NFTs. If you want to make 3 offers for 1 ETH, you will need 3 ETH, because for each offer 1 ETH will be blocked in your wallet. When using WETH, you will only need 1 WETH for all 3 offers and a bit of ETH for the gas fee, because your 1 WETH would go to the first offer that has been accepted and the other two offers will be automatically canceled if you don't have enough in your wallet. Since only about 10% of offers lower than the selling price will be accepted, you don't have to wait until your offer runs out before you can do the next offer. Even with a small amount of WETH you can make multiple offers without risking that you overspend your cryptos.

So, let's buy your first NFT! After connecting and funding your wallet you need to search for a very low-priced NFT (< 0.015 ETH) from a verified collection, just to try out the purchasing process for fun. You can use the "Stats" menu => "Rankings" and sort by floor price to find a cheap NFT with a blue verified badge, for example, Moonling or Yolo Holiday are listed at the time of writing for around 0.01 ETH. After you have decided on an NFT you like, the next thing to do is to buy your NFT. Be aware that OpenSea is the secondary market most of the time, so it is like the eBay version for NFTs.

The primary sale often happens through minting on the project's website, and you need to make sure you are on the right one because there are many fake websites that look similar to the original website. Once you connect your MetaMask wallet to one of these fake websites and confirm the message in your MetaMask wallet, you will lose everything in your wallet or—if you are lucky—you will just send your precious Ethereum to the scammer's wallet, but never receive anything back. Also, be aware that you often pay more for the transaction fees than what you pay for a cheap NFT. But don't worry, we'll stick to OpenSea for now.

You can also go to the "Explore" menu on OpenSea to see the different types of NFTs that the marketplace offers. Browse the different categories to get familiar with the offers. Beginners should only buy from verified accounts or collections—they are marked with a blue checkmark to the right of the name. Make sure when you hover your mouse over the blue checkmark, it shows the message "This is a verified account" or "This collection belongs to a verified account..."

There are several options for buying:

- Buy now: pay the price the NFT is listed for
- Make an offer: you can make an offer for a lower price than listed or for NFTs that are currently not listed for sale.
- Dutch auction: The price will decrease with the auction time period and the person who makes the first bid will purchase the NFT
- English auction: The highest bidder during the auction time period will get the NFT.

Congratulations! Now you have your own NFT. What next?

Keep It Safe!

Although just three words, it is one heck of a task. A lot comes into play to keep your NFTs safe and secure. Notice how we talked about securing your crypto and NFTs even before talking about how to buy them? That's because it's so important.

You must keep your NFTs safe. Even before you get an account in an exchange, you open a wallet account or choose an NFT marketplace. Safety should be your watchword. In the NFT space, there are many scams to be wary of. We hope you know that NFTs are not perfect, and we'll talk more about that in chapter 9. Reading about all the different scam systems in that chapter can save you a lot of money and emotional pain.

In the next chapter, we will give you an overview of popular NFT marketplaces.

Chapter 5: Investing in NFTs (Directly)

If you want to begin investing in digital collectibles, assets, art, and tokens, we recommend you take your time to study the different strategies that are possible. One strategy can be, of course, to directly purchase single NFTs of promising projects (that we will mention further down in this chapter). But can you rely on NFTs as a long-term investment?

Many investors lack basic knowledge about NFTs and have no clue what they are buying if they don't take time for detailed research. It's like investing in a particular company's stock, just because the price is constantly rising without having any background information on the company's business model or why the prices are rising. The most crucial step for new investors to take before entering the NFT industry is research. There is no difference between buying NFTs or stocks and bonds—first, you have to understand what you are getting into.

Here is an overview of what types of NFTs were mostly traded in the second quarter of 2022:

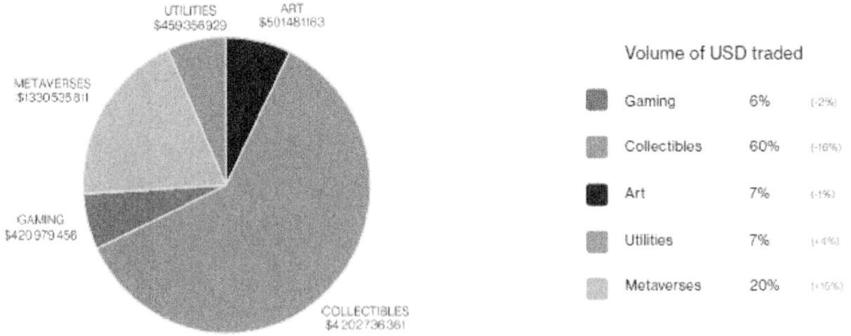

Image 11 Quarterly NFT Market Report Q2/2022

NFT profile pictures such as CryptoPunks are also in the category of collectibles. Art in the traditional sense only makes up 7% of the market in USD.

Could the NFT market crash? Of course, anything is possible, but so could the stock market. In fact, in July 2022 the NFT market shrunk by 94% since the beginning of that same year.

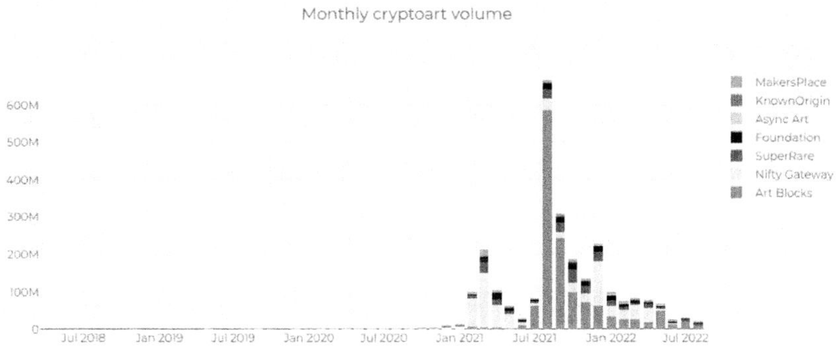

mage 12: Montly cryptoart volume (without Opensea!) by Cryptoart.io [46]

Nevertheless, after the significant drop, the hype has calmed down and we are seeing some prices slowly rise again. Also, since the price for buying Ethereum is currently at acceptable levels again, it might be the perfect time to get some of the established NFT projects if you have some spare money to invest.

Here is an overview of the most profitable projects in the second quarter of 2022:

Segment	Project	Total Profit / Loss	Total Profit	Total Loss	Average Profit at Resale	Rate of Resale at Profit	Average Ownership Duration
METAVERSES	Otherside	$300,343,059	$377,621,801	$-77,278,742	$4,427	89.3%	2.73
COLLECTIBLES	Moonbirds	$224,757,668	$250,419,190	$-25,661,523	$14,331	93.0%	2.73
COLLECTIBLES	Bored Ape Yacht Club	$132,799,222	$386,151,347	$-253,352,125	$49,730	58.3%	75.85
COLLECTIBLES	Azuki	$35,835,970	$132,503,708	$-96,667,738	$8,410	65.7%	18.00
UTILITIES	Ethereum Name Service	$32,362,384	$37,158,423	$-4,796,039	$52	98.1%	9.42
COLLECTIBLES	Goblin Town	$26,784,432	$34,671,198	$-7,886,766	$1,234	83.1%	2.41
COLLECTIBLES	Doodles	$26,399,898	$56,538,906	$-30,139,008	$12,133	67.6%	46.84
UTILITIES	Proof Collective	$21,933,132	$24,446,906	$-2,513,774	$94,390	79.9%	70.81
COLLECTIBLES	Phantom Network	$14,929,489	$36,301,003	$-21,371,514	$1,881	75.3%	3.37
COLLECTIBLES	Chimpers	$11,749,901	$14,415,054	$-2,665,153	$1,792	90.2%	2.33

Fig. 13 – Performance of the top 10 most profitable projects – Q2 2022

Image 13: Performance of the top 10 NFT project in Q2/2022 (by nonfungible.com)[47]

If you don't have the time or the motivation to do hours of research, but you still want to participate in the coming boom of NFT applications, you could choose an indirect approach by investing into the infrastructure and service providers for NFT technology. For example, you can purchase stocks or cryptocurrencies that will benefit from the coming NFT boom (see chapter 8).

And, of course, another (and the best way) of investing in NFTs is to use them in your own business. NFTs can boost your business or project if you are in the music industry, in the publishing business, if you have a fashion brand, a sports team, if you work in health care, government, charities, philanthropies, or nonprofit organizations, if you are in the video game industry, or even a cultural institution. Think about how you can use blockchain technology somehow for your own business to improve customer relationships, marketing, or internal processes.

Why Invest in NFTs?

Why pay for an NFT when you can see and display the image or video for free? This is a typical question that people who don't know very much about NFTs will ask. Apart from the technical reasons that prove the ownership and scarcity of an NFT on a blockchain, there are many more reasons to invest.

It could be that the artwork actually has meaning to the owner. It could be that the owner identifies with the artist's work or is touched by their story. Or you are just an NFL fan and enjoy collecting cards of your favorite players. There could be a useful utility of an NFT such as in-game items, domain names, virtual land, or access to an exclusive community where you get insider information or where you can participate in the decision-making of a project (DAO). For some people, a reason to buy an expensive NFT could be prestige, for example, to show off being able to afford an Ape. Since NFTs are documented on a blockchain, everyone can look at what you have in your wallet address. Other people just enjoy hunting and collecting things.

But are NFTs a good investment? There is no better way of answering this question than by looking at the potential gains and losses of those who have invested in NFTs. This way, you can make more informed decisions and know where to put your money. As with any other investment, putting your money into NFTs gives you the chance to accrue revenue as the investment matures. Before starting this book, you might have been surprised that some NFTs have sold for jaw-dropping amounts. In the fine art world, the works of established, well-known artists have demand and are more likely to gain value than the works of a newcomer artist without any representative. However, if the newcomer artist becomes famous, the value of their works will explode.

NFTs' values increase only if their popularity increases. So, if you acquire an NFT at the beginning of a project, you'll be in luck when it gains popularity, and you can resell it for huge profits. Famous projects like CryptoKitties, Bored Apes, and CryptoPunks turned out huge profits for their early investors. The good thing about NFTs is that they can be bought and sold by anyone from anywhere there is a computer and Internet, while fine art is limited to certain galleries and auction houses.

If you're a seasoned investor, NFTs present a way for you to diversify your investment portfolio. With an NFT, you are getting an alternative to your traditional methods of investment, and you stand to make great profits when the NFT increases in value in the future. Since in 2022 we have a huge bear market, it might be a good time to pick up popular projects at a bear market price. Apart from that, digital assets are the future, so investing in NFTs will provide you with ample opportunity to learn and gain valuable knowledge about crypto assets and blockchain technology. It is expected that anyone willing to put money into new technology will at least research it, and this research will help broaden your knowledge about digital art and other emerging technologies.

Here are some questions to consider before you make a purchase:

- Who is the creator of the NFTs? Is it one single person or a group of people?
- What have they created and sold so far?
- Do they follow a unique, authentic style?
- What is their long-term vision? Do they have a roadmap?
- Does the NFT have a use? Are there any additional perks?
- How many followers do they have on different social media channels? How regular are they posting and when was the last post on social media? If there is no post for the last 6 months, maybe this project will cease to exist.
- How responsive is the artist or team about your questions?
- Who else is collecting the project? Are NFT whales collecting the NFTs? How many unique owners does the NFT collection have?
- Does the project have funding from investors? Is there enough money to continue the project long-term or if there are problems like being hacked and losing substantial amounts of money?
- Are you happy with holding this NFT, even when the price might drop in the future and never go up again?
- Can you put into words why you like this project?

Where to Buy NFTs - NFT Marketplaces

Now that you know how to be a good NFT investor and how to buy NFTs, let's see where you can buy NFTs. Before picking a particular NFT marketplace, we recommend looking at each of the marketplaces below to see what resonates with you. Do you like their user interface and the information they provide? What fees are they charging and in what (crypto) currencies can you pay? How many users use the marketplace? What is the user activity on each marketplace? Do they sell a lot every day or a little? Do you think this marketplace will survive the crypto bear market and continue to exist?

If you intend to use the NFT marketplace, it's important to pick the right one. They often specialize in a particular area or niche. We have prepared for you an overview with relevant information to make your marketplace choice easier.

OpenSea	www.opensea.io

OpenSea is currently the largest NFT marketplace with over one million users in 2022 and over 80 million NFTs on its platform. As far as NFT sales are concerned, OpenSea leads the rest. The platform boasts a wide range of different digital assets, and you don't have to pay anything to sign up and navigate through the wealth of assets put up for sale. Furthermore, it allows creators and artists to create their own NFT by providing an easy minting process on its platform. Its support of almost 200 different payment tokens gives credence to its name. If you're just starting out in the NFT industry, OpenSea is the best place to begin.

Pros	Cons
• easy user interface with many filter options • creators can easily mint tokens without having to use the blockchain • transparent listings based on sales volume • easy swapping ETH in WETH (wrapped Ethereum) • responsive customer service • you can pay via credit card	• free minting but when you sell, they charge a 2.5% transaction fee • error messages are common • over 80% of the free NFTs created on OpenSea are fraudulent or spam

Coinbase NFT	nft.coinbase.com

Coinbase crypto exchange has also opened its NFT marketplace, which looks similar to OpenSea.

Pros	Cons
• easy user interface • no minting for everyone • comment function on NFTs • Follow functions like on social media	• Ethereum only • there is no transparency over the platform's user activity, we assume it is still low

Nifty Gateway	niftygateway.com

Nifty Gateway has been instrumental in selling many famous digital artists like Beeple and musicians like Grimes. The platforms' NFTs are called Nifties, and they're built in Ethereum. It's probably the most exclusive and heavily curated NFT marketplace out there. If you are a long-term NFT investor, you will find great deals here that can last for a long time.

They also show their NFTs on other platforms such as OpenSea. You can find NFTs of celebrities such as Deadmau5, Eminem, and Paris Hilton.

The marketplace is controlled by Gemini, the crypto exchange which is in turn powered by the Winklevoss twins. The art curation marketplace allows you to trade NFTs in Fiat money like US dollars, unlike its counterparts that insist on cryptocurrencies.

When you purchase NFTs, the platform hosts them for you against the standard practice of allowing you to hold the NFT in your wallet. For many collectors, this is not in tune with how flexible they want their digital assets to be.

Pros	Cons
• you can pay in dollars with your credit card without buying cryptocurrencies first • curated and verified drops • invitation only for artists, art curators check everything • free minting • good customer support	• free minting but when you sell, they charge a 2.5% transaction fee • no good statistic filters to see sales volume and activities on the marketplace

Rarible	rarible.com

Rarible marketplace features different types of NFTs, the same way that OpenSea does. But where OpenSea allows different cryptocurrencies for exchange, Rarible accepts the marketplace's token called Rarible.

Rarible is modeled on the Ethereum blockchain. You can buy and sell digital art, collectibles, music, and videos on the platform. Rarible has gotten some great companies to invest in it.

They focus on popular NFT collections, mostly profile pictures. If you mint on Tezos, you can save a lot of money on gas.

Pros	Cons
• has a "lazy minting" feature like OpenSea's • easy to explore various sellers and trending collections • has a follow feature like social media, which helps you get notified about new drops from your favorite creators • supports Ethereum, Polygon, Solana, Flow, Immutable X, and Tezos, and they are planning to integrate more blockchains in the near future • low fees: Rarible takes 1% on the buyer side and 1% on the seller side from every sale on the marketplace	• free minting but when you sell, they charge a 2.5% transaction fee • error messages are common

SuperRare	www.superrare.com

A curated marketplace that focuses on single-edition (= super rare) digital art, photography, paintings, films, and 3D imagery.
Just like Rarible, SuperRare also provides a platform for various kinds of art to be traded. Both Rarible and SuperRare NFTs can be traded on OpenSea.
Rarible requires that collectors use Ethereum to buy whatever artwork they want. The marketplace offers digital creators a platform to sell their videos, 3D images, and art.
In a recent statement, SuperRare announced that it now has its own token bearing its name based on the blockchain. It intends to use the tokens to build new digital creators for its marketplace.

Pros	Cons
• quality artwork • strong community • easy user interface largest trade volume of all exchanges	• they only work with ETH for all transactions, which has high gas prices • 3% transaction fee for all purchases, paid by the buyer • 15% of primary sales • no good statistic reports for sales volume and activities

MakersPlace	www.makersplace.com

MakersPlace has specialized in curated motion art, animation, and cinematography. Only verified works are displayed. They partnered with auction house Christie's to sell Beeple's Everydays-The First 5,000 Days for $69.3 million.

Pros	Cons
• easy user interface • you can pay via credit card • you can see the marketplace's activity • you can like and comment on NFTs like on social media	• very high commission of 15% • only supports Ethereum blockchain • low sales volume

NBA Top Shot	nbatopshot.com

Are you a basketball enthusiast? Then the National Basketball Association and Women's National Basketball Association marketplace is just for you. This marketplace uses the Flow blockchain, created by Dapper Labs (the creators of the CryptoKitties) to store the NFTs, but you can pay in Ethereum on their marketplace. It has a large community and offers memorable highlights, moments, and videos from the NBA.

Pros	Cons
• easy user interface • good customer support • you can pay in dollars with your credit card without buying cryptocurrencies first	• you cannot trade the NFTs outside the marketplace • the Flow blockchain's ecosystem is not as large as Ethereum's • targets a very specific fan base which limits the circle of potential buyers

Mintable	mintable.app

Famous entrepreneurs Mark Cuban and Marc Benioff back this marketplace. They have integrated Ethereum and MetaMask wallets and offer a gasless system for minting a token.

Pros	Cons
• no fees to mint	• fees are the same as OpenSea, but they have less traffic • only supports Ethereum blockchain

Axie Infinity	marketplace.axieinfinity.com

This marketplace was specifically created for the video game Axie Infinity, which was inspired by the Pokémon game. The game had more than eight million users in 2021. You can buy and sell NFT game characters, in-game land plots, and artifacts. Since 2020, there has been ongoing hype for this game for the simple reason that it is founded on a play-to-earn model. It is very popular in the Philippines, Vietnam, and Thailand. Strangely, on their marketplace, you cannot pay in their own Axie token (AXS) but only in Ethereum.

Pros	Cons
• the game has an attractive play-to-earn model	• you cannot trade the NFTs outside the marketplace • this marketplace is only for Axie Infinity's in-game tokens so anyone outside their ecosystem might not be interested in their marketplace • simple graphical user interface • this year the game is struggling to gain new users • according to Forbes, the game is showing signs of a pyramid scheme[48]

OneOf	www.oneof.com

This marketplace has partnerships with eBay and Warner Music Group. They are using Tezos and Polygon blockchains which have a much lower cost than Ethereum.

Pros	Cons
• you can pay in dollars with your credit card without buying cryptocurrencies first • you can pay in Tezos, Bitcoin, USDC, Polygon, and Ethereum • they claim to be a green, energy-efficient NFT platform	• fees are the same as OpenSea, but they have less traffic • only supports Ethereum blockchain

KnownOrigin	knownorigin.io

Based in Manchester, UK, this marketplace features only select artists. Although founded in 2018, eBay announced in June 2022 that they are acquiring the KnownOrigin marketplace.

Pros	Cons
• high-quality art • activity history of the marketplace available	• high fees, 15% of primary sales • only supports Ethereum blockchain • strict access to the platform as an artist

Binance NFT	www.binance.com/en/nft/home

Binance is the world's largest cryptocurrency exchange and has launched its own NFT marketplace. You can use the Binance Smart Chain (BSC), the company's blockchain, which greatly reduces gas fees on the platform by allowing users to pay with its native Binance Coin (BNB).

Pros	Cons
• extremely low minting cost • more than 800 digital artists • more than 300,000 NFTs • trusted and secure platform provider • well integrated into Binance Exchange platform	• high fees • low royalties for artists • their ranking and stats are not as good as on OpenSea • navigation through the marketplace feels overwhelming

Foundation	foundation.app
Small marketplace focusing on fine arts, digital art, photography, and 3D art. They sold the notorious Nyan Cat and works by the artist Pak.	
Pros	**Cons**
• easy user interface • build a personal feed by following your favorite creators • better quality art for higher prices	• high service fee • low daily volume • sales history of items cannot be seen easily • no good search filters • Ethereum only

Art Blocks	www.artblocks.io
This is not really a marketplace, rather a platform that curates generative art. Generative art refers to work that has been partially or completely created using an autonomous system. Here you won't find goofy animal profile pictures. Launched in November 2020 by Snowfro and other curator team members, they have attracted many interesting artists.	
Pros	**Cons**
• easy user interface • build a personal feed by following your favorite creators	• low daily volume • sales history of items cannot be seen easily • Ethereum only • choice of music seems very limited

Async Art	async.market

Async Art is an NFT marketplace for art and music. For artists, they offer a dynamic creation tool feature in which you split a digital painting into a Master NFT and "Layers," and then you can randomly create a unique combination depending on the rarity you define for each layer. Art that can evolve over time, react to its owners, or follow a stock price is now all possible with programmable art. Because of that, you won't be able to distribute NFTs on other marketplaces. They also list their NFTs on OpenSea.

Pros	Cons
• easy user interface • purchase process is on OpenSea so you will be familiar with the process • well-curated NFT selection • a lot of NFTs have clear license labels	• no good filters

Theta Drop	www.thetadrop.com

This NFT platform specializes in decentralized video and television distribution. Theta Drop has its own blockchain and cryptocurrency (THETA and TFUEL). They partnered with the World Poker Tour and some celebrities such as Katy Perry.

Pros	Cons
• easy user interface • you can pay in dollars with your credit card without buying cryptocurrencies first	• only TFUEL tokens are accepted as crypto • no minting tools for creating your own NFTs

Magic Eden	magiceden.io
This Web3 marketplace specializes in NFTs on the Solana blockchain, but you can also pay in Ethereum. On their launchpad, you can see upcoming NFTs for minting. Holders of their own NFT "Magic Ticket" will get access to their DAO on Discord where you can receive rewards and influence the development of the platform.	
Pros	**Cons**
• easy user interface • strong Solana community • launchpad feature • watchlist feature	• offers a lot of plagiaristic content and rip-offs of popular projects

VeVe	www.veve.me
VeVe is a marketplace that has specialized in 3D model NFTs, mostly from popular comic books and movies (Superman, Jurassic Park, Batman, etc.)	
Pros	**Cons**
• many popular characters available	• only on mobile phones available

There are more marketplaces, but we believe we covered the most important ones. There are also marketplace aggregators such as GEM where you can bulk buy, but this is not for beginners, yet.

NFT Marketplaces For Music Lovers

Audius	audius.co

Audius Web3 streaming and sharing platform was launched in 2019 with one goal: putting power back into the hands of content creators. Artists are able to distribute their music free of charge, and the team states that it will always be free for artists. The platform has a rewards system that pays artists in $AUDIO tokens.

Pros	Cons
• easy user interface • free for artists • attractive revenue system for artists • upload music immediately	• no minting feature

Async Art Music	async.market/music

Async Music is the music-focused part of the NFT platform Async Art. Instead of using different layers within an image to create unique combinations of the layers as NFTs, artists can upload audio layers that make up a song (beats, bass, vocals, percussion). This allows for offering dynamic music that randomly changes parameters each time you listen to a song. The platform is curated and doesn't allow open minting.

Pros	Cons
• professional look • random music NFTs are possible • curated collection	• dynamic feature is complex • not easy to use for beginners who want to list their music here • only 17 songs currently available • no clear information on what user license comes with each track

Sound.xyz	www.sound.xyz

They combine streaming with minting and community listening. Artists can launch a listening party for new songs via NFTs. To get your music listed on this platform, you need to contact one of the established artists on the platform because it works via invite-only. Or you can join their Sound Discord server. The platform is currently still in beta.

Pros	Cons
• easy user interface • daily listening parties • many collections sell out • artists keep 100% of the proceeds generated by the sale	• no clear information about what user license comes with each track

Catalog	beta.catalog.works

On this website you can add your music for free live streaming and set a "buy now" price. Music buyers can also make an offer for a song. However, the platform is currently invite-only. The platform is currently still in beta.

Pros	Cons
• easy user interface • artists receive 100% of their initial sales • artists set the resale price they want to receive themselves	• no clear information about what user license comes with each track • long onboarding process because there is only a small team behind

Emanate	info.emanate.live

Emanate is an Australian-based private company that offers a Web3 music streaming platform built on the EOS blockchain. It uses its $EMT tokens for payments and rewards artists for every stream, while its competitor Audius only currently employs the rewards system for artists to earn crypto. The platform is currently still in beta.

Pros	Cons
• easy user interface • anyone can list their music	• no clear information about what user license comes with each track • NFT sales link to OpenSea

Opus	opus.audio

Opus is based in the UK and promises decentralized music distribution and streaming using InterPlanetary File Systems (IPFS) on the blockchain. Users listen to music through smart contracts, which provide a way for users to compensate creators for their music. They are using the Ethereum blockchain, but for payments, they are using their own OPUS token (OPT). Users might receive a share of royalties in exchange for creating playlists that help spread music throughout the platform.

Pros	Cons
• modern user interface • high royalties for artists	• not possible to see if they have active users. Seems to be in Beta.

NFT Marketplaces For Physical Art

By now, we assume you have seen several uses of NFTs you never before knew and how to make money from them. But what if you are not a digital artist? You are creating beautiful sculptures, prints, or paintings—things you can touch and smell. Are you left out? The answer to that question is no, of course not. Digital art benefits the most from NFTs, but that doesn't mean physical art cannot be sold as NFTs as well. For instance, the German fine art auctioneer Van Ham organized the first NFT auction in Germany on the 1st of December 2021. The auction witnessed the sale of hybrid NFTs, where an NFT accompanies a physical artwork, and they sold well.[49]

There are NFT marketplaces that have specialized in hybrid NFTs to help artists to be also successful in the digital world.

misa.art	misa.art
A small marketplace focusing on fine art that they try to sell via NFTs. They want to bridge the gap between the traditional art world and the crypto world.	
Pros	**Cons**
• easy user interface • build a personal feed by following your favorite creators • better quality art for higher prices	• high service fee • low daily volume • sales history of items cannot be seen easily • Ethereum only

Another website that we would like to mention here is Courtyard (courtyard.io). Courtyard is not a marketplace for NFTs, but they help to give physical collectibles and eCommerce products a new life by producing their NFT counterpart using state-of-the-art 3D rendering of products.

What Are the Top NFTs to Invest in (2022)?

The best part of dealing with NFTs is choosing the right ones and the best projects that will help you achieve your investment goals in the long run. With every passing day, there are thousands of new NFTs coming onto the market and hundreds of new projects appearing. But how do you sift through the trash to find the right ones? Which projects are the most promising and worthy of your money? What should you look for in a project?

The NFT space moves really fast, what happens in one month in the NFT world might be one year in real life. The constant flow of great new ideas and art makes it increasingly difficult to stay up to date with all the launches and news on Twitter and Discord.

Therefore, we have created the ValueBird NFT community, in which we exchange recommendations and important news for people who are interested in NFTs. You can join our free Telegram channel if you want condensed NFT news:

t.me/valuebirdnft

Alternatively, you can join us on Twitter **@TheValueBird** (**www.twitter.com/TheValueBird**) to get selected NFT news without being spammed.

If you want to succeed in your NFT journey, then research is something that you should grow accustomed to. Once you see an NFT you like, the next step is conducting thorough research about the project. You will have to know everything about that project, from who created it to its communities and the project itself.

Don't just choose NFT projects from random people. You will have to research how well they have done in the past with other projects or if it is their first time. Also, check what people have to say about them. See if they can properly execute an NFT project, their level of brand awareness, and of course, their social status. Once you see a creator performing well in the above qualities, then you might have just landed yourself an NFT project that is fit for holding onto for a long time. The project, or better put, the brand, is what attracts people and retains its demand. When researching an NFT project, you must consider the project's branding. If it can draw you to the project, it can draw more attention from you and other NFT enthusiasts. Go for brands where you enjoy what they do and like what they represent. If you don't enjoy what they offer, the project is not for you.

A good NFT project will not just have good brand qualities, but also will have a very healthy and supportive community. Things to expect from such communities include,

- positive vibes
- regular communications from the creators covering alerts, updates, and technical help
- active members who are willing to help out

Since the crypto and NFT market dropped 80% in 2022, a lot of people are afraid that all the NFTs might go to zero. Therefore, in 2022 we have seen a trend to concentrate on only established projects. We would like to mention some blue chip projects that have not lost their supporters during the bear market in 2022, and most likely should bring capital gains in the future for long-term holders. Remember, before buying any of these, you need to analyze them yourself—this is not financial advice. That being said, here are some NFT projects you must have heard of and that are considered blue chip NFTs:

CryptoPunks

CryptoPunks have gathered much popularity because of the ever-recurring record-breaking sales. The CryptoPunks NFT projects began in 2017 by Larva Labs, inspired by the London punk community, the cyberpunk group, and electronic music stars like Daft Punk. Several Punks from their collection have been sold for millions. They seem to have a loyal and wealthy fan base, just as the Bored Apes collection has. The demand for CryptoPunks is high because they were the first NFTs to be introduced on Ethereum and have therefore entered a new chapter of digital art.

Meebits

Created by the same people as CryptoPunks—Larva Labs—Meebits are traded for a much lower price. There are 20,000 unique Meebits characters created that look like Lego dolls. Clearly, the success of Larva Labs' earlier project, CryptoPunks, radiates to their following projects. But the Meebits can be seen as the next step from 2D CryptoPunks to 3D Meebits that can be used as Avatars in metaverses in the future. The owner of a Meebit will also receive an OBJ file, which is the full 3D model of your Meebit that can be imported in any standard 3D animation software. You can easily animate your Meebit then and let them perform any actions you want.

Autoglyphs

To cover all of Larva Labs' collections, we would also like to mention Autoglyphs. Autoglyphs are the first "on-chain" generative art on the Ethereum blockchain, which means the art itself is not stored on a separate file server, but really fully on the blockchain. Originally created in 2019, they were available to anyone who was willing to donate the creation fee of 0.2 Ethereum. We bet you wish you donated that amount now because the floor price on OpenSea is now at 229 ETH. There were only 512 glyphs created, and after that, they can only be purchased on the secondary market. The generative algorithm is capable of creating billions of unique artworks, wrapped inside an ERC-721 interface. Because this was probably the first project of this kind of art, it is unbelievably valuable now. The same can be said for CryptoPunks.

Bored Ape Yacht Club (BAYC)

This collection, created by Miami-based Yuga Labs, consists of 10,000 Apes with unique traits. They were sold for a primary price of 0,08 ETH—bet you also wish you'd bought one of these! The current floor price is usually not lower than 80 ETH at the time of writing. The good thing here is that owners also have full commercial usage rights, which is hardly the case for other NFTs, unfortunately. Being an owner, you will receive regular, exclusive perks and have access to official merchandise articles. If there is an NFT that you absolutely have to own today, it would be one of the Bored Ape Yacht Club collections. Yuga Labs went from launching an NFT collection with a mint price of 0.08 ETH (or $210) to a leading Web3 brand valued at an impressive $4 billion in a little over a year. We believe whenever you see prices bottoming, it might be worth grabbing one of their NFTs. To have one of these in your wallet will be your access key to a very exclusive community, comparable to a very exclusive golf club. However, be aware of exceptionally low prices—there are many forgeries on the market because of their popularity.

Mutant Ape Yacht Club (MAYC)

This is another Yuga Labs collection of 20,000 apes, which were originally given as a present to holders of the BAYC NFTs. You might catch one for less than 10 ETH, but considering holders of a BAYC NFT received them for only a gas fee makes them a precious gift for BAYC collectors.

CryptoKitties

CryptoKitties is a blockchain game around breed-able, collectible, and kind of adorable kitties developed by Canadian-based Dapper Labs (the same that created the FLOW blockchain and NBA Top Shots marketplace). In the game, players try to raise cats with the rarest attributes, which have a higher value on the market. By now, there have been more than two million CryptoKitties minted, and the floor price is therefore quite low. You can maybe buy one to experience the process of an NFT purchase if you have not bought an NFT yet.

Azuki

Released by a Los Angeles-based group of artists, this collection of 10,000 anime-themed avatars sold out in less than five minutes and made over $29 million. Soon, the floor price went above 10 ETH and reached about 40 ETH at its peak. Currently, the floor price is around 8 ETH, but sales volume on OpenSea is still high, which means demand for Azuki NFTs is still excellent and you will be able to sell them quickly. Owning an Azuki grants the user access to exclusive NFT drops, streetwear merchandise, live events, and more.

CLONE X

This collection has reached a considerable market capitalization and focuses on high-end avatars for a metaverse. The current floor price for the 20,000 NFTs is around 7 ETH. Behind the project is RTFKT (pronounced "artifact") in collaboration with famous Japanese designer Takashi Murakami. RTFKT has been working on NFT sneaker projects for Nike and was eventually acquired fully by Nike in December 2021. The future plan of this project is to build a game and metaverse.

Moonbirds

Another financially successful pixelated profile picture collection is Moonbirds by media company Proof. There are 10,000 Moonbirds available, and the lowest floor price is now down from its high of 38 ETH in May 2022 to around 14 ETH. They come with private club membership and additional benefits the longer you hold them. The team behind them claims that they are building a metaverse and holders of Moonbirds will have first access to it. If you can't spend 14 ETH on a Moonbird, you can try their much cheaper Moonbird Oddities, which are a derivative of Moonbirds. The good thing about Moonbirds and Oddities is that they have moved to a CC0 license, which means "no rights reserved" on intellectual property. Anyone can use them for commercial use without copyright restrictions.

Doodles

This is a collection of 10,000 hand-drawn profile pictures that could easily grow into a Hello Kitty-style brand in the future. Owning a Doodle allows you to vote on community-driven features, products, and events. The community can decide on future developments of the brand, and their Doodlebank community treasury boasts over $5m USD to fund the implementation. The lowest floor price is now down from its high of 24 ETH in May 2022 to around 7 ETH. Congratulations if you were one of the lucky people who minted some for 0.123 ETH.

Chromie Squiggle by Snowfro

Another successful collection by Art Blocks founder Snowfro are the Chromie Squiggles. There are currently 10,000 Chromie Squiggle NFTs featuring unique, randomly generated squiggles of color. Originally sold for only 0.25 ETH, their record sale so far was from a buyer who bought two Chromie Squiggles for $4 million (1,362 ETH). The current floor price is around 10 ETH, but it peaked at 14 ETH in July 2022.

Invisible Friends

With impressive 500k Twitter followers, this NFT project of Swedish animator Markus Magnusson has become an outstanding collection. The intention of the creator is to focus on clothing and accessories instead of characters. Only 5,000 NFTs were created, and the floor price is only at 2 ETH (coming down from 7 ETH). As part of their roadmap, Invisible Friends is collaborating with streetwear fashion brand KITH to sell limited, luxury streetwear to their communities. With impressive 500,000 Twitter followers just for Invisible Friends, this should be an easy sale. Unless Elon Musk was right about the high number of fake Twitter profiles...

Justin Aversano - Twin Flames

His 100 NFTs in the Twin Flames collection have gained huge popularity in the NFT scene and lucky are the early birds who bought it for 0.55 ETH after minting. The current floor price is 68 ETH; however, sales do not happen very often, as we can see on OpenSea. The photos feature twins from all over the world in honor of his own twin brother who had passed away. The pictures capture the essence of being a twin, as Justin said himself.[50]

Again, since he was the first mover in his space and the first NFT portrait photographer ever on a blockchain, he is able to achieve premium prices for his work. Justin keeps the original prints, which at some stage he will show in their entirety in a museum one day. A smart move, we think. Will he share his profit from that showcase with his NFT owners?

Damien Hirst - The Currency

For those on a lower budget, we can point you to the famous British artist Damien Hirst, who has created 10,000 small oil paintings since 2016 showing colorful dots on a mousepad size canvas. In July 2022, NFT owners could register on a special website and decide if they want to burn their NFT and receive the physical artwork or if they want to have their physical counterpart destroyed and make their NFT 100% unique. About 40% preferred to have the physical artwork and the remaining 60% kept their NFT. An exciting and clever marketing move. Many buyers, therefore, bought 2 NFTs—one to keep and one to own a physical edition of. Damien Hirst has been selling his works for millions of British pounds over the past years. Hirst's most provocative work, which made him famous, was a shark preserved in formaldehyde in a clear display case. The amount paid for the shark is undisclosed, but for sure it was a couple of million.

VeeFriends

Within a very short period of time, VeeFriends has become an influential NFT collection on the market. The amount of money this project attracts is incredible, all due to the omnipresence of its founder Gary Vaynerchuk (also called Gary Vee) in nearly all NFT social media channels. He owns several social media and marketing companies and is a bestselling author. He also organizes the world's biggest NFT conference, the VeeCon, once a year, where you can meet the high society members of the NFT world. Holding a VeeFriend NFT is—you've probably guessed it already—an entrance ticket to the VeeCon and therefore very popular. He also announced plans to open the very first NFT restaurant "Flyfish Club" in New York in 2023. To gain access to that restaurant for you and up to five people you need to have the right NFT in your wallet. To explain all his activities and projects, we could write a whole chapter in this book, but we prefer that you start doing your own research about Gary's projects because he is also a visionary and trendsetter in the NFT world.

Cool Cats

Cool Cats are a collection 9,999 of randomly generated NFTs from over 300,000 total combinations of outfits, faces, and colors on the Ethereum blockchain. The mint price was 0.02 ETH, and the floor price now is 2.5 ETH. They are part of their Cooltopia ecosystem and are key to earning the $MILK tokens that can be used across Cooltopia. The cheaper version in their ecosystem are Cool Pets NFTs. The aim of the project is to create a gamified NFT experience, and owning a Cool Cat NFT grants you evolving access to games, tokens, community events, collaborations, and more.

To find more lucrative projects, you can always use the stats functions on a marketplace. Additionally, in our NFT tool chapter further down, we will give you tools that support your research. Also, pages like CryptoRank help to find the blue chip NFTs:

RECENT PERFORMANCE OF TOP 10 NFT COLLECTIONS BY MARKET CAP

Excluding lands, arts and utilities. Data source: NFTgo

NAME	MARKET CAP	FLOOR PRICE	7D FLOOR PRICE CHANGE	7D AVERAGE PRICE	7D VOLUME
CryptoPunks	$2.31B	⧫ 67.49	+1.49%	⧫ 67.09	$3.59M
Bored Ape Yacht Club	$1.79B	⧫ 72.6	+4.18%	⧫ 77.46	$14.2M
Mutant Ape Yacht Club	$772M	⧫ 12.36	+3.08%	⧫ 14.46	$6.82M
Meebits	$682M	⧫ 3.5	+3.24%	⧫ 3.79	$1.35M
CLONE X	$503M	⧫ 6.9	+10.6%	⧫ 7.21	$2.90M
Moonbirds	$415M	⧫ 13.5	+2.23%	⧫ 13.94	$2.08M
Azuki	$348M	⧫ 8.4	+25.4%	⧫ 8.46	$3.64M
Doodles	$261M	⧫ 7.4	+7.39%	⧫ 7.47	$1.57M
VeeFriends	$185M	⧫ 5.93	+6.08%	⧫ 6.71	$253K
Bored Ape Kennel Club	$164M	⧫ 6.95	+10.5%	⧫ 6.93	$1.54M

CryptoRank.io @CryptoRank_io @CryptoRankNews Aug 26, 2022 CRYPTORANK

Image 14: Top NFT collections according to Cryptorank[51]

Summary of Top NFT Projects

As you might have noticed from our list above, many successful collectible projects have offered a relatively cheap mint price. Since they earn around 10% royalties with every sale, they are still participating in later increased prices. By continuously building value for their community, these projects have earned their high floor prices.

The Best Metaverse Projects for NFT Investments

Since NFTs will play an essential role as digital assets in upcoming metaverses, you are probably wondering what top metaverses are worth your time researching.

A metaverse is a persistent, virtual world. As we mentioned before, there is no single metaverse. When people talk about the metaverse, they talk in general or refer to a specific one, because every company is trying to build its own metaverse and there is currently no connection between the different platforms. In the far future, connections between them might be developed so users can communicate via different metaverses. However, we are not sure about this, since, of course, every platform is aiming to keep its users engaged as long as possible in the world they control.

A metaverse differs from a video game in that its structure won't be linear, and players will be able to explore the virtual world freely.

Since Facebook's company rebranded to Meta, many metaverse projects suddenly received more attention and investment capital. Actually, Facebook and other social media platforms are already a metaverse, a virtual world in which people meet and communicate, but not built in a 3D virtual reality. The next logical step would be to create a virtual 3D world in which people can learn, play, or communicate via their avatars without ever needing to leave their houses. Ideally, the future platforms will be decentralized, and users will benefit from sharing their data. Meta's upcoming metaverse will most likely not be a decentralized metaverse, but a centralized world like Roblox. In the midterm future, you might not buy your food in a supermarket but in a metaverse, and you will be able to see every product in 3D and read the label.

Most current metaverses offer a SDK (software developer kit) which everyone can use to create something on the virtual land you purchased: houses, avatars, items, games etc.

We have created a guide book about the top metaverses coming in 2023, which you can download for free on our bonus page:

www.thevaluebird.com/bonus/

Strategies for NFT investments

There are some general investing rules for Cryptos and NFTs that we would like to share. First of all, don't invest money in NFTs that you are not willing to lose. Never risk any money that you need to get back in a few months because it might be the wrong time to sell your NFTs or cryptos. Never borrow any money to invest in cryptocurrencies or NFTs.

Depending on your willingness to take risks, only put 1 to 10% of your total investment portfolio into cryptocurrencies and NFTs. There are plenty of other good investments out there, so don't put all your eggs in one basket. And from that amount you choose for your NFT/crypto budget, don't put it all into one project. Spread the amount within the asset class as well.

The thing with cryptos and NFTs is that there is currently no backup system, and there is no insurance if a marketplace goes bankrupt or if there is a hack, or if you send money to the wrong wallet address. We know many people who became millionaires from investing in cryptocurrencies and NFTs because the profit margins can be insane when you get in and out of a project at the right time. But we also know people who have lost a lot of money. And if that money was supposed to pay your rent next month, you have a problem. For sure, anything can happen to an NFT, the collection, or a project. Prices can skyrocket within a few days or can plunge in a twinkle of an eye.

So, if you are going to be investing in NFTs, then you need some strategies. The right strategies will help you to have a less stressful, more enjoyable NFT investment journey.

There are several strategies for NFT investments. A popular one is the flipping strategy, in which items are bought at low prices and sold quickly for a profit. This strategy works well in bull markets (when prices are rising constantly). Especially after launching a project, there is general media hype, so you can typically sell your NFT within a few days for double the price you bought it for. However, you would be terribly upset if you bought a Bored Ape at 1 ETH and sold it for 2 ETH while discovering a year later that the price is 60 ETH. Therefore, depending on the project, a long-term buy-and-hold strategy, in which you also benefit from free airdrops, is more advisable.

Collectors and investors focus on the long-term performance of their NFTs, similar to traditional art. Long-term strategies require more expertise in each project and of course a bit of luck in finding the next shooting star. Famous NFT collectors are Mark Cuban, Gary Vaynerchuk, Metakovan, Gmoney, and Pranksy. On their Twitter profiles, you might find their wallet address ending in .eth or .nft. You can search for this address in OpenSea or a blockchain explorer to get insight into what they hold.

Of course, you can combine the flipping and long-term strategies, depending on the popularity of a project. Although you'll probably make the most profit by making your own NFTs for your business. If you are a business owner or a creator, think of how you can add value for your customers by using NFTs.

Let's look more closely at some of those NFT-buying strategies.

Flipping NFTs

As mentioned before, flipping means buying items at the lowest prices and then selling them quickly for a bit of profit. Here you need high volume, and you won't hold onto your NFTs for long because the art itself and its creators are less important. Many investors are looking at the floor price and imagine themselves becoming rich without having sold their NFT at all. To actually be profitable, you need a buyer who is willing to buy your NFT. Maybe you have seen a project where the floor price has increased by 100%. However, be aware that the holders can set the floor price. They can always place their NFT on the marketplace for whatever price they want. That doesn't mean it is a real market price. Therefore, we always check the volume and sales history, because if the volume has not increased, the chances that you can sell your NFT are slim.

Also, verify if there are new buyers. New buyers will reflect how much demand there is for a project. Only demand ultimately causes the floor price to go up, not the asking price of the holders. High volume means that there are many new buyers flowing into a project that might increase the price further in the future. Looking at the sales volume of a project, you also need to check if you are dealing with a bull market (daily sales volume increases) or a bear market (daily sales volume decreases). You never want to flip in a bear market when prices are going down and down. You can use tools like www.nft-stats.com, Nansen (www.nansen.ai), and CryptoSlam! (cryptoslam.io) or the OpenSea activity tab. If you are unsure if the volume will go up or down, you might want to wait for one or two more days to confirm it. It's like trading on a stock market: you never want to guess the bottom, because it can always go lower.

Start with low prices of 0.2 ETH or less to practice. When you sell your NFT, set the sales price for 0.999 ETH instead of 1 ETH, because it will not just look cheaper, but also your listing will be listed before all the 1 ETH offers. A very simple human behavior sales tactic. Unless you got on a whitelist, avoid buying a project the first days after a launch because there is usually a lot of hype, which pushes the price up. And never buy at the top, wait for the hype to calm down. Analyze which NFTs in a collection have rare traits. You can use rarity.tools for this or check on OpenSea on the collection page—you have trait category filters that you can open and then filter for the NFTs with rare traits.

As a rule of thumb, the trait should be fewer than 100 NFTS, the less the better. The ones that have fewer than 20 are too expensive and less liquid. You want to stay near the floor price, or, if you can't find a rare one, then only buy the floor price. It should be either the lowest price or a super rare find, nothing in between. All the liquidity is at the floor price. Anything in between will be more difficult to get out of without selling at a discount. As a rule of thumb, buy 99% the floor and 1% rare.

Another method to grab an NFT for a low price is to make lots of offers lower than the floor price. And we mean a lot of offers—less than 10% of your offers will be accepted. Your offer must be higher than the last offer made of course, and it should not be too far from the asked price, a maximum of 15% lower, to have a chance to be accepted.

These are the basics of the short-term flipping strategies, but you make more profit when holding long-term.

Long-Term Holding (HODL)

HODL is a term derived from a misspelling of "hold" meaning buying and holding cryptocurrencies. It also stands for "hold on for dear life" among crypto and NFT investors, meaning not selling when markets go down or become volatile. If you hodl the right NFTs, you will gain higher profits. CryptoPunks and BAYC needed two years to climb so high in price, and other projects or artists might need 5–10 years to become equally popular. To be successful, you might consider the following advice:

Don't Buy Derivatives

An NFT derivative is an NFT project utilizing the creative assets and the intellectual property of an already existing project.[52] For example, there is an unofficial Doodles derivative called "Lil Baby Doodles X". Many unofficial NFT derivative projects tend to be cash grabs created without the intention of building a long-term community or retaining value. There can also be official derivatives of a successful project's founders to satisfy the need for ownership of new market entrants at lower prices. But can you name one successful project that is a derivative of another project? We can't.

Don't Copy Trading Influencers

Social media influencers have many different reasons to tweet about a project other than to help you, ranging from paid promotions, exit liquidity dumping, or just pumping their own wallets. Money corrupts everything, therefore, always do your own research, and watch the volume and prices before you go in. Come up with your own system, and never follow others blindly.

Don't Trade at Night

When trading under stress or in the middle of your bedtime hours, mistakes are made quickly. You placed a fat finger offer of 0.3 instead of 0.03 ETH or you confirmed a scammer message too quickly in your MetaMask wallet. Do you want to ruin tomorrow? The NFTs are not running away. Go to bed, sleep, wake up, and place a trade when you are not under time pressure. The price tomorrow might be even lower than yesterday.

Don't Trade Emotionally

When trading, aim to be in a calm emotional state. The moment you start feeling FOMO (fear of missing out), greed, boredom, excitement, or frustration, close your computer and go for a walk. Your emotions will corrupt your mental state and prohibit you from thinking clearly. Any sort of emotion will cloud your judgment. You might search OpenSea for hours and hours looking for the right NFT, but you can't find it. And that is okay. Don't force yourself to buy anything just out of boredom or frustration. You can never lose by sitting on the sidelines, and there will be new chances to get into your favorite project at lower prices later.

Do Your Research

NFTs are relatively new, so they are a prime target of scammers. A lot of fraudsters have created projects to rug-pull and scam investors. Evolved Apes and Frosties are some of these projects. These two projects managed to rug-pull investors up to $3 million in NFT value. Therefore, always take your time to study the project you would like to invest in and do your due diligence and a background check. Don't buy an NFT you don't know anything about or have not done substantial amounts of research on. Before you buy anything, ask yourself "Why will this project be more valuable in 6 months?" This simple question is perhaps the most important. If you can't answer it clearly, join their community, ask questions, and see how the response is. Is their community real, or only fake profiles and bots?

You can use special tools to do your research and keep track of your NFT investment and journey. We'll talk about more of those tools at the end of this chapter. Also, follow NFT creatives and projects on Twitter, Discord, and other social media platforms. Observe the activity on their pages, as these clue you into whether their project will be a hit or just another NFT project there to cash in some quick cryptos.

Instead of picking trending NFTs for a quick flip, it is better to pick projects developed by established artists, as these projects hold the better promise of gaining value in the long term. Also, it is easier for these projects to attract venture capital for their growth.

Join the Whitelist

As we mentioned before many blue chip NFT projects were minted at low prices, below 1 ETH. But depending on the project launch process, not everyone can mint an NFT. The first spots are given to loyal community members that are on a so-called "whitelist" (sometimes also called "allowlist"). The time period when the minting takes place is announced to the people on a whitelist, often even before the official minting launch date (also known as a "drop"). To get on a whitelist, it is important to purchase popular NFTs at low prices. In general, participants who can secure a whitelist spot sell their freshly minted NFTs at higher prices, but there are also cases of projects with less popular demand, and the NFTs get cheaper after minting in the secondary market. However, according to data culled from OpenSea, people who participate in the whitelisting processes make over 76% more profit than those who are not whitelisted.[53]

Whitelists have several benefits. It helps creatives and creators reward those who support their work early. It also helps to reduce high transaction fees and avoid gas wars. You usually can also mint 3–5 NFTs in a single transaction while paying the gas fee only once. To get on a whitelist, you will need some information from the project creators' Twitter or Discord server. It often requires engagement in their Discord servers and promoting their project by inviting new members to their social media channels. Social media influencers can often easily score a spot. Other projects use riddles or games as an entry requirement for their whitelist. Be aware that you often don't know what particular NFT within a collection you will acquire during this process, as the details and images are often revealed after the minting. After the whitelist sale, the public sale will start until the collection is sold out. If you want to flip the NFT fast, you need to calculate how much gas fee you paid and add this to your desired profit as well as the selling fees of the marketplace.

NFT Renting

This is a relatively new opportunity in the NFT space, and another strategy for investing in NFTs. NFT renting allows you to make money from your NFTs without selling them. This is mostly applicable to in-game NFTs, intellectual property, and digital real estate. In-game play-to-earn items can be used by other users to either level up or boost their fighting chance. The reason this is possible is because of smart contracts. As you already know, these contracts hold the deal and agreements that bind you and the player renting your NFTs. You can choose your renting period, rate, and any other necessary arrangements. Or if you have a membership NFT, but you are not using it, you might want to rent it out, such as the NFT for Gary Vee's upcoming exclusive Flyfish Club restaurant, which requires guests to hold an NFT in order to reserve a table. One platform that allows for NFT renting is reNFT (www.renft.io). It allows users to lend and rent NFTs.

NFT Staking

As we described in chapter 1, you can stake your cryptocurrencies to earn more cryptocurrencies. This is quite common in the cryptocurrency space. But did you know you can also make money from NFT staking?

NFT staking is possible because of the merger between Decentralized Finance, DeFi, protocols, and the NFT's technology. It means locking up or depositing your NFTs in a DeFi smart contract to earn rewards. It is a beneficial way to profit from your NFTs without selling them. NFTs have become even more attractive due to this possibility of passive income.

On several platforms, you can stake any NFT you have, but on others, you can only use their NFTs. Here are some platforms that allow you to stake NFTs for rewards:

- NFTX (https://nftx.io/)
- Kira Network (https://kira.network/)
- Splinterlands (https://splinterlands.com/)
- Polychain Monsters (https://polychainmonsters.app/defi/staking/)

- Onessus (https://whenstaking.com/stakes)
- Band NFT (https://bandroyalty.com/staking)

Curator Strategy

If you are not an artist and don't plan to spend all the work and effort to create your own NFTs, it can be a good strategy to become an NFT curator. It would be similar to the strategy that people use on Instagram: they are either content creators or content curators. Content curators search for the best content on the platform to pick the best for their followers. For example, a vegan recipe profile could show you the most interesting vegan recipes every day to inspire what you cook next. You don't have to spend all the time buying the ingredients, preparing the food, filming everything, and cutting and editing the video to provide content. You just ask permission from content creators to post their material and they are usually happy to share their work on your profile to get more exposure. Once the curator has acquired plenty of followers, they will monetize their account with advertisement posts.

You also do this as an NFT curator. Instead of just hunting for money and buying everything you come across, you could only pick art that fits into your collection. Few collectors follow this strategy at the moment, which you can see from the mix of NFT types they hold in their wallets.

What type of art or collectibles are you interested in? You could only invest in photography, music, or generative art, for example. Create a name that reflects the theme of your collection. Maybe you collect only comic book characters or movie-based NFTs, or perhaps only artwork that has a certain dominant color. How about funny NFTs or NFTs that support a charity? Or maybe you only collect images of celebrities that are wearing a Rolex watch. Those photos will always resell well.

There are so many possibilities on which you can build your collection's identity. Get a Web3 domain for your curator name and open a Twitter account under the same name. Then, post every time you make a purchase and why you added this NFT to your collection. If you are the very first collector in your theme, you have a lot of opportunities to build a large following before other people have the same idea. Now, the number of NFT collectors is still small compared to Instagram or TikTok. Later, when there will be 500 vegan NFT art collectors, it will be a lot harder. And you never know, if later a new collector wants to get into your niche, you might get a fantastic offer to sell your whole collection because he or she likes your collection and trusts your expertise.

NFT Investment Summary

When it comes to holding traditional fine art or NFTs, think long-term, think many years. For example, knowing what you know now, if you bought Bitcoin at $30 and sold it at $900—do you think that was a good deal? Think in 10-year cycles. The big money is made when you hold your real estate or your fine art or your Apple stock for 10 years or longer. Meanwhile, you enjoy cash flow from renting out your property, lending your art to a museum, and collecting dividends from your stocks. When prices have seemed to form a bottom, it is time to get in, not when prices are skyrocketing. As the saying goes, "scared money don't make no money." If you take no risk on your capital, there will be no returns on your capital. However, only take calculated risks, and invest money that is not important to you.

How many digital wallets do you think currently hold NFTs? We found different answers to that question and were unable to verify a correct number, but according to Findstack.com there are approximately 29 million wallets holding NFTs in 2021, while other resources stated much lower numbers.[54] But let's assume 30 million is more or less the number of wallets holding NFTs right now, and be aware that active collectors have more than one wallet. How many people live in the world? That means only a tiny fraction of people in the world are in the NFT market because we are still in a very, very early stage. Don't underestimate this market. This is not going to stay a small nice forever—just look at what happened with Bitcoin.

Use These Tools to Increase Your Profits and Navigate the NFT World

Doing your research for NFT investing can be quite time-consuming, but it is essential to invest successfully in NFTs. Aggregated data, statistics, and good filters assist in better assessing an NFT. Within the same collection, some NFTs sell for millions while others are not even making a few hundred dollars. Why is that? The answer to that question lies in the rarity of an NFT. To support you in your investment decisions, we have collected several helpful tools for you. Still, it's up to you to double-check the data provided on these websites, and blindly trust what they display. We never know how they earn their money...

NFT Trading Tools

rarity.tools	www.rarity.tools

Ensure you do adequate research on valuable upcoming NFTs by utilizing this rarity analytic tool.

NFT PRICE FLOOR	nftpricefloor.com

A very useful tool that we also used for research on this book. You can see the floor price history of NFT collections, which helps assess whether the current price is low or high.

NFT Catcher	www.nftcatcher.io

This website helps you to see what new projects will be launched so you avoid missing a new drop. If creators could get their project launch listed here they might get more attention.

Ayzd	ayzd.com

This website helps you to learn about the NFT & metaverse projects. It also has a drop calendar.

DappRadar	dappradar.com/nft

Discover the hottest NFT collections, marketplace rankings, and top real-time sales.

Trait Sniffer	traitsniffer.com

Trait Sniffer is a metadata calculation tool that calculates a rarity ranking based on the trait distribution that an NFT collection has within seconds after the reveal. Useful for new NFT traits projects and collecting valuable NFTs right after the reveal - even before officially updated on Opensea.

Trait Sniper	www.traitsniper.com

Trait sniper helps you to see rarity rankings very quickly after a project is revealed.

NonFungible	www.nonfungible.com

Not really a tool, but they provide useful analytic reports about the NFT market. However, it seems they do not use any data from Opensea.

NFTGO	nftgo.io

Another NFT analytics platform for Web 3.0, NFT and gaming communities. Spot NFTs by ranking, rarity and they offer a drops calendar (https://nftgo.io/nft-drops)

NFTEXP	nftexp.io

Read the latest NFT news. They have an asset explorer, which didn't show any sales however.

NFT Stats	www.nft-stats.com

This website shows the last 24 hour top NFT collections ranking from various marketplaces and a rarity explorer. They also source NFT community statistics directly from Twitter and Discord.

icy.tools	icy.tools

Another analytics tool to track NFTs across marketplaces. They provide a good minting overview as well.

NFTNerds	nftnerds.ai

Here you can also check rarity information and rankings. They claim to have all data in their site and you can buy with auto-triggers when a token matches your filter criteria.

Moby.gg	moby.gg

Alert tool that checks mints, sales and popular wallets.

Crypto Slam!	cryptoslam.io

This is a popular NFT collection ranking site by sales volume.

NiftyRiver	www.niftyriver.io

This is a popular NFT collection ranking site by sales volume. You can also check mints filtered by different blockchains.

Art Blocks	www.artblocks.io

A small marketplace focusing on fine art that they try to sell via NFTs. They want to bridge the gap between the traditional art world and the crypto world.

There are also interesting Twitter accounts such as Spr3adsh33t (https://twitter.com/spr3adsh33t). They are bot developers that search on Discord to give Statistics for NFT investors and traders.

We recommend having a look at each tool to see which one you prefer the most. Usually the paid ones deliver better data than the free ones.

Token Trackers

What are token tracker tools? These websites help to view details of each transaction and wallet. You can enter the wallet address or the smart contract address in a search field and then you can see all the tokens held in this wallet and the transaction history. This is very useful for analyzing where the money flows, whether a transaction was successful or not, or to identify possible fraudsters.

Etherscan	etherscan.io/tokens-nft

This is the official token tracker website of Ethereum. This is basically a pair of glasses you can put on to see everything that is happening on the Ethereum blockchain. Under the menu "Resources" => "Charts & Stats" you can see interesting statistics for the Ethereum blockchain. Very insightful to see where the most traffic goes as well. Once you use this tool you will understand how transparent blockchain technology is.

Polygonscan	polygonscan.com/tokens-nft

This is the official token tracker website of Polygon (MATIC). Thankfully the developers made this page very similar to the Ethereum Scan website so you will find the same data in the same position. Under the menu "Resources" => "Charts & Stats" you can see interesting statistics for the Polygon blockchain again.

Solscan	solscan.io/nfts

This is a Solana token tracker website made by a Singaporean private company. You can find all the data that is captured on the Solana blockchain.

Nansen	www.nansen.ai

Nansen is a professional analysis tool that you need to pay for. They claim that more than 100,000 investors are using their tool to get valuable crypto and NFT data.

Dune	dune.com/home

Dune is a free crypto analytics tool where everyone can create their own custom charts if you know how to code. In the dashboard you will find many pages by other developers that you can use as well. If you filter for the dashboard tags you can quickly find interesting data analysis.

Genie	www.genie.xyz

Another ranking website that aggregates data from different marketplaces. You can also move your NFTs for sale from one marketplace to another and you will pay less gas fees when using their website.

NFTBank	nftbank.ai

NFTBank is an NFT portfolio management tool that will also help you to keep an overview of the total value of your NFT collection and also with tax filing.

WGMI	wgmi.io

Another NFT portfolio management tool is WGMI. It comes with a news feed. You can get lifetime access by buying their NFT.

Zerion	zerion.io

Zerion also helps you to manage your DeFi and NFT portfolios and to trade across different networks. You have to create a Zerion wallet and download their app on your smartphone, which we do not recommend. We recommend buying, selling and managing your NFTs only on a desktop computer or laptop.

Other Useful Tools

Google Trends	trends.google.com

With Google Trends you can check what people are searching for over a defined time period. You enter up to 5 search terms to compare which ones are more popular. You could search for 2 or 3 popular NFT collections to find out which one has higher search volume on google.com. This also helps to identify general trends, for example if you search for "NFT" you can see the general people's interest in NFTs.

Fees Tool	fees.wtf

When you link your wallet to this tool, it will show you how much gas fees you have paid since you started trading NFTs.

Ethereum Gas Fees	ethereumprice.org/gas/

Remember that the Ethereum gas fees are usually not fix? The amount of gas charged for each transaction depends on how complex the transaction and how congested the network is. This website will show you the gas price chart of Ethereum and also a table where you can see what times the gas prices are low or high during the week. The chart is not in ETH currency, the Ethereum gas price is measured in so called "gwei". Gwei is a denomination of the cryptocurrency Ethereum network. Gwei is also called nanoether, because one gwei is one-billionth of one ETH. When you buy low priced NFTs it is often worth waiting until gas prices will be lower.

NFT Pirates	nftpirates.io

This website is offering a bidding robot that bids for example automatically on a % based below the floor price. No need to spend hours overbidding other bots manually anymore.

Nexo	nexo.io/nft-lending

This is an NFT lending platform where you can borrow up to 20% of the value of your Bored Ape Yacht Club or CryptoPunk without selling them. They will only accept collections worth more than $500,000.

CloneMyNFT	www.clonemynft.com

London bases software company offers a cloning service for your NFTs which allows you to keep an NFT clone in your wallet after you sold your original NFT. It will look identical but the origin of the NFT is missing. You could even sell this clone if you find a buyer for it.

Chapter 6: Easily Create and Sell Your Own NFTs in 5 Steps

The digital assets market is booming, and NFTs are not being left out. Digital creators and artists make millions from selling their digital art. This is a breath of fresh air, a welcome development for the digital community whose works are hardly appreciated and constantly plagiarized. The advent of NFTs has helped reduce the plagiarism and copyright infringement issues that digital artists have to contend with. With NFTs, an artist's work can be shared, and the record of the artist's ownership can be stored in the blockchain. This way, the ownership of any artwork can be traced and verified on the blockchain.

The digital art and NFT boom has attracted many people to the community, including you. This detailed step-by-step guide shows how to mint and sell an NFT, just as we promised.

To create or mint your own transferable NFT you need to follow a certain standard of the Ethereum token, and you need to follow the standard of the marketplace you want to sell.

Before we had NFT marketplaces, where creating an NFT is easy for anyone, you had to have a working knowledge of smart contracts and the programming language Solidity. Using Solidity, you can create your own smart contract for NFTs and then deploy it on any blockchain for the later minting of your non-fungible tokens. This was and still is a very technical process for programming experts and not, for novices. Beginners can now use the simple minting feature called lazy minting offered by OpenSea and other marketplaces. This way, you don't need to go through the technical process of using the Solidity programming language.

We recommend you open a few popular, blue chip NFT projects on OpenSea that we presented in chapter 5, and that you study how they structured their metadata. In our example, we use the OpenSea marketplace since it is the most popular one.

Step 1: Identify the Art or Digital Item to Mint your NFT

Minting an NFT simply means converting a digital item to NFT. You can't mint NFTs if you don't have digital items to convert. So, the first step is to choose the digital item you want to mint, for example, a high-quality image, text, audio, or video file. Technically, you can use any kind of digital file and list it as an NFT, but if you want to use the lazy minting feature, each marketplace only supports certain file formats. Once you have identified the digital item you want to mint, you can move to the next step.

One important factor to consider is the transaction fees, which may lie beyond your budget if you want to sell several thousands of NFTs on the Ethereum blockchain, which has high, fluctuating gas fees. Before you list your collection for sale, wait until the gas fees are low. Typically, the fees are lower late at night and in the early morning. In the tools chapter, you will find two websites that help you to find the best times for low gas fees. Alternatively, using Solana or Polygon blockchain will have significantly lower fees, but NFTs on these blockchains have also lower sales volume than NFTs on Ethereum. In your price calculation, don't forget, you also have to pay OpenSea 2.5% of the NFT price when it sells.

Step 2: Install MetaMask Wallet

In chapter 4, you should have already set up your MetaMask wallet. There are many cryptocurrency wallets you can use for storing your NFTs. If you are a beginner at setting up wallets, we recommend using MetaMask. You might want to use a different wallet address than the one in which you hold your NFTs for investing. This can be done very easily by clicking on your account profile (circle image on the top right) and then you select "+ Create Account." Also, to be more transparent to your audience, we recommend you register your minting wallet with your artist name, for example, myartistname.crypto on unstoppabledomains.com. That way everyone can easily look back and see that you minted the NFT. Also, enter that wallet name in your Twitter and Discord profile, so everyone can see your official wallet name. You can check our Twitter profile as an example:

Oftentimes, there are sudden pop-ups asking to be granted access to your wallet. If you have already connected your wallet, be careful! This might be someone trying to access your assets, and you must decline the request. It is always better to read everything twice before accepting any wallet requests.

Step 3: Choose an NFT Marketplace

After you have picked a digital item to mint as an NFT and have set up your MetaMask wallet, the next step is to identify a dependable NFT marketplace that will mint your NFT. There are various NFT marketplaces, from Mintable to the popular OpenSea. You can browse through a variety of them in Chapter 4.

For the purposes of this book, we will be using the OpenSea marketplace to mint our non-fungible Tokens. To begin, a sort of authentication is required. This is where your MetaMask wallet comes into use. You'll use it for authentication, after which you're now ready to mint your NFT.

Step 4: Mint your NFT

Minting your NFT is pretty straightforward. However, you could get lost if you're not properly guided.

The first thing to do is create an adequately named collection in the OpenSea marketplace. Click on your top right profile image, then on "My collections." Ensure that you give it a proper name and a captivating description. The description is very important and allows you to include important information about your NFTs. If you want to offer two or three different themed NFTs, for example, vector graphic profile pictures that resemble different birds and your collection of funny cat photos, you should also create two separate collections with good descriptive names for each collection. The collection name, ideally, somehow relates to what you are offering in that collection.

Before minting your NFTs, you need to create a collection, and it contains the following metadata:

	Mandatory	Optional
Logo Image • 350 x 350 pixel logo image that will represent your collection.	✓	
Featured Image • 600 x 400 pixel image is not shown on your Opensea page unless Opensea decides to feature your collection. You really should upload one professionally looking, because being featured by Opensea will drive serious traffic to your collection.		✓
Banner Image • Upload a catchy, professional looking 1400 x 350 pixel image to give collectors a good impression. If you don't have one, hire a graphic designer on Fiverr.com who can make a logo, feature and banner image in one order to support a homogeneous branding of your collection.		✓
Name • must be a unique name on Opensea	✓	
Opensea URL • customize opensea URL to your collection, for example https://opensea.io/collection/valuebird		✓

Description

- We see many collections lacking a good description, which is a wasted opportunity. Banner, logo and description is your shop window, so describe the purpose of your collection in max. 1000 characters. What inspired you to create this collection? What is the story of this collection? Who is the creator and what is his/her work experience? How is the money generated from this collection being used? Hire a good copywriter maybe if you want to boost your NFT collection. You can also add certain syntax to create headlines, bold or italic text style, for example **the best cat photo collection** will show the text between two stars in bold letter. ✓

Category

- The category (art, music, collectibles, utility) will help to make your item searchable by category on OpenSea when people browse a certain category. Each collection can have maximal 1 category assigned. ✓

Links

- Add links to your website and social media channels so your audience can find you there. This helps to grow your followers on different social media. ✓

Creator Earning

- This is the groundbreaking part of NFTs. Creators can add here a wallet address where to receive automatically ongoing royalties and the percentage of how much to charge for each resale (usually no more than 10 %). The fee set here will apply to all NFTs in this collection. Unfortunately, Opensea does not show to potential buyers what the set royalty fee is. Be aware that if someone sells your NFT on a different marketplace the royalty fee might not be paid if sold on different marketplaces than where the NFT was created. ✓

Blockchain

- Select the blockchain where you'd like new items from this collection to be created by default. Ethereum is the most common one, ✓ but currently still has the highest gas fees. Polygon and Solana would have much lower gas fees. This setting cannot be changed later.

Payment Tokens

- Here you can select multiple tokens that can be used to buy and sell your items. We recommend selecting as many as possible because sometimes it prevents buyers from ✓ making an offer if they don't have the right token in their wallet and they would need to exchange tokens first to be able to make an offer or a purchase.

Display Theme

- You can choose between 3 different layouts ✓ for your collection.

Explicit Content

- Activate this setting if you want to sell ✓ sensitive content

Don't worry if you do not have all the details ready. You can still edit and change your collection images, links, and description after creating it. Only the blockchain you want to use cannot be changed. You can also delete a collection and create a new one.

After you have created your collection, you can start creating your first NFT. Click on the "Create" menu in the top right and you will be asked to provide the following data:

	Mandatory	Optional
Image / Main Content • Here you need to think about the purpose for which the token was created and add the content, for example a digital artwork, a domain name or virtual land. The content would be an image file, music file, video file, gif or 3D model. If you are selling a domain name, you would add an image with the domain name in it as a representation. For digital land, it would be the exact location of the plot within the virtual world (metaverse). The main content could be nearly any file format, however, the allowed file format depends on the marketplace you are going to use. Opensea currently supports these file types: JPG, PNG, GIF, SVG, MP4, WEBM, MP3, WAV, OGG, GLB, GLTF. Also check the maximum allowed file size, which is on Opensea 100 MB.	✓	

Name • Of course your baby needs a name so people can search for it. You may want to add an edition number "(1/100)" or "1 of 100" at the end of the name. This would communicate to customers that the NFT is number 1 in an edition of 10. If you only have 1 edition you can add the number for each NFT, for example "Doodle #1234". • After the image it is the first what people look at and read so use your name wisely to stand out in the marketplace	✓	
External Link • OpenSea will include a link to this URL on this item's detail page, so that users can click to learn more about it. You are welcome to link to your own webpage with more details.		✓

Description / Perks

- Write a detailed description of what you are offering, including what the unlockable content is, copyright or trademark information or, if any, other included perks for the buyer. Also we would mention the number of editions and how many tokens there will be in your collection. You can also add a link to a license contract or terms and conditions.
- This field is perfect to explain what the perks are for the buyer. Perks are additional advantages you will offer, for example a free ticket to your next concert, to meet the artist at the next event or a physical product that can be redeemed on a website. The link to that website should be in the unlockable content, not here in the public description. You can also include special conditions for the perk, such as an end date for the offer or until the owner needs to hold it. Perks are great to increase the value of your NFT. How awesome would it be to meet the artist?
- If you include valuable perks make sure you auction these for a higher price, because perks usually only go to the first buyer (unless it was not redeemed by him or her). Alternatively, you could say the perk goes to whoever owns the NFT on a specific date. To avoid disappointments of your customers make clear the rules and we advise to make it transparent somehow which NFTs has redeemed its perk and which hasn't (on your website for example).

Collection

- Here you select the collection you created before from the selection list. If you don't select one the NFT will show up directly under your profile.

Property Traits • you can define for each NFT what attributes or traits they have. This is very important for in-game items or trading cards. You can create them in free text and organize them in trait types/categories. For example, for in-game items you can create the types "Weapon", "Gear", "Shields" and then create different properties in each type. A rarity level (1-10 or 1-5) can help buyers to filter for the most rare NFTs in your collection, for which you can charge more of course.	✓
Level • numerical traits that show as a progress bar, see Property Traits	✓
Stats • Numerical traits that just show as numbers	✓

Unlockable Content

- Only the owner of the NFT can see this content. It increases exclusivity and adds value because you offer more content than just the digital asset. You can include information in the public description of what the unlockable content is or you keep it as a surprise to raise curiosity. It could be more files (images, videos) or a contact information / website for redeeming a physical product, an online training programme, a note from the NFT creator or a free ticket to a special event. In Opensea the unlockable content is only text so you have to add an external link if you want to provide more files. The file should be password protected to avoid that the link is being shared in Discord groups. If you want to keep it simple you can also provide a special perk email in which someone can email you with their name and address and their wallet address which you can then verify if they hold any of your NFTs. ✓

Supply

- The supply is usually 1 which makes your NFT unique unless you want to create several copies of the same. For editions (number 1 of 100 editions) the supply is still 1, because each NFT has its unique, sequential number, for example #1 / 100 ✓

Blockchain

- Select which blockchain you would like to use. ✓

Step 5: Sell your NFT

You have created your NFT, but you have not yet minted it on a blockchain. Don't sell your NFTs until you're done listing your complete collection by adding all the individual NFTs to that collection, because the moment you sell the first NFT on OpenSea, the entire collection goes onto the Ethereum blockchain. If you want to add more NFTs later, it will cost extra ETH.

Double or triple-check everything before you sell because selling will freeze your metadata, such as the title, description, and properties of the NFT. This is because serious buyers want security that the listing will not change after they buy your NFT. You can only delete and re-mint, but that costs extra gas fees if you use Ethereum.

After creating your NFTs, the next step is to mint and sell your NFTs. After all, that's the reason for all your hard work! You click on your top right profile image, which should show you all your NFTs. You can then either select a single NFT and then click on the blue "Sell" button or click on the three dots ... (more options) of one NFT in the overview page, which opens a menu, and select "Sell." That way you can multiple select several NFTs and sell them in one step for an identical price. You are going to need some Ethereum to pay the gas fees.

There are three options you can choose for how you set a price for your NFT, either a fixed price or a timed auction. If you select the auction process, you have two options to choose from again, which are either sell to the highest bidder (English auction) or sell with a declining price (Dutch auction). For both, you select a starting price. For the Dutch auction process, you want to start at the highest possible price you think you can achieve, and the price will count down until it reaches the ending price. OpenSea will automatically lower the price until the end date. The Dutch auction takes advantage of people's fear of missing out because if potential buyers wait too long, someone else will seize the item and end the auction.

For the English auction, you will start with a low price that still covers all your expenses. As you might know already from eBay, in an English auction, the starting time period is usually very quiet, as potential buyers don't want to cause rising prices too early. So don't be disappointed because bids might pour in towards the end in an English auction. You can start another auction without any problems if the auction ends without a buyer.

On OpenSea you can never increase the price of your NFT. You can only lower it. If you really need to raise the price you have to delete the listing and relist—both actions require gas fees. Start with the highest price you think anyone could possibly be willing to pay—but also keep it as low as possible—so you cover your cost. Remember, if your collection becomes popular, you will receive plenty of royalties from each resale.

We'd love to tell you that that's the end of the process, but it's not. Buyers wouldn't just flock to your NFT because you found a way to mint a digital item. You need to woo them. You need to market your project to potential buyers. This process isn't as hard as it might seem. You can use Twitter, Instagram, and Facebook to create ads targeted to your audience.

Depending on how compelling the ad is and the beauty and description of your NFT, you can garner buyers almost immediately. There are different ways and strategies for selling your NFTs, which you'll discover in the next chapter.

But how can you benefit from NFTs if you are a physical artist? How do I turn my paintings, sculptures, or printed photography into an NFT? First, you will have to convert your physical art into a digital version (photo or video). There are several things you will have to consider while doing that. What strategy would you like to follow to sell your physical art? There are several options possible:

- You can choose to sell both the NFT and the physical art separately.
- You can either sell the NFT with the art or sell the art with the NFT.
- You could let the customer decide if they want to destroy the original art and keep the NFT only.
- You could let the customer decide if they want to burn the NFT and keep the physical art only.
- You can also sell the NFT while the art is still in the creation process

After you have decided which option to give your customers, create high-quality photos or videos of your artwork and use these in the process above to mint your NFTs.

Voila! That is all it takes, and your art can now be sold as an NFT. However, digital artists have a clear advantage here. They don't have to think about the many options, since there is only one digital artwork, and they often speak to a different audience than collectors of physical art.

Chapter 7: Strategies of Successful NFT Sales

So far, we've covered a lot about NFTs, from how to buy one to how to create one. Now, it's time to talk about how to sell one successfully. The NFT market has skyrocketed since 2021, but bottomed in 2022, and we know it is not easy in such a large market to launch a new project. But on the other hand, the technical barriers are lower than ever before with OpenSea and other marketplaces offering easy minting functionality. Remind yourself every day that you are still very early in this market, and if you invest your time in it, it can be worth it in a few years. Above all, after reading the first chapters of this book, you already understand perfectly what an NFT is, which puts you miles ahead of your competition. Remember, Beeple didn't sell his art for $69 million within a week. He had to deliver consistent results to his audience every day for about 13 years until he made this record sale and became famous as a digital artist.

Don't attempt to earn quick cash. Remind yourself that finding collectors for your NFTs requires value, patience, persistence, and convincing social media marketing. Refrain from spamming your fans—let your art speak for itself. The key to the promotion is your artwork!

What is your story?
What is your why?

And just because your art is great and speaks to itself, don't feel guilty for running a marketing campaign on social media. Your work requires constant promotion because every day new NFT projects are being launched—you need to stand out in all that noise. Don't see a promotional campaign as a sale, consider it as a way to inform your community. Many investors are keen to invest their money in good projects that will continue to thrive in the future. They are always checking their social media accounts for new, trending collections and upcoming artists.

The secret of successfully selling your NFTs requires you to build your NFT and artist brand and communicate its rarity. Your NFT must be desired, nothing else matters. When an item is unique, it is more valuable than other items that are not considered valuable. Take, for instance, the Mona Lisa painting, displayed at the Louvre in Paris. Wouldn't you like to go and see the best-known, the most visited, and the most parodied work of art in this world? Louvre tickets sell better because of its rarity and fame.

Therefore, the story around why you created the NFT has to be communicated to the artist's audience. For your NFTs to sell, they have to stand out from other NFTs. They must be more unique or offer more value than any other NFT rising at that particular moment. Once the story behind the work is clear, building a strong relationship between your NFTs and its potential buyers becomes important. There are plenty of online communities (we'll list some later) dedicated to minting and selling NFTs and many of their members are extremely supportive of each other. Show your NFT collection to some people in these groups and get some feedback before your launch. You might be surprised by some great advice that makes a big difference.

Be mindful of transaction costs. Polygon, Tezos, and Solana are cheaper than Ethereum. You might start your first collection on one of the cheaper blockchains to learn the complete process and build your community.

Keep in mind, it might take days, months, or maybe years to sell your first NFT. There is no overnight success for any business, entertainer, or celebrity, although you might hear a lot of these stories in the NFT space. Just because you drop an NFT doesn't mean that someone will magically find it and spend money on it. A lot of hard work happens before a project becomes successful.

Also, your existing reputation does not automatically convert to your NFT creator reputation. We have seen many celebrities with more than a million followers who cannot get a single bid on their NFTs. We have seen artists with excellent physical art sales history, but flop in the digital landscape. Selling NFTs is complex, no matter who you are. With the right marketing strategy, you can create a collector base first that is willing to support your output long-term. And since you will earn a percentage from every resale, you can build a supplemental revenue stream in the future.

Create Roadmaps

Before even creating your NFTs, you should have a roadmap to guide you through your NFT journey. A roadmap will help you define the strategy and plan using milestones to help you achieve your NFT goals. Where do you see the project in the next six months, in one year, and in two years? How much do you think your NFT would be worth then? Would your NFT be a series? When would the next item in the series or collection be ready for sale? All of these factors should be considered in your roadmap.

A detailed roadmap helps indicate transparency and show how committed you are to your goals and objectives for your NFTs. If you don't know how to create a roadmap for your NFTs, look at the road maps of successful NFT brands and learn from them.

Avoid Copying Successful Projects

Extremely successful NFT projects attract many copy-cats, even similar art designs. Have you noticed how many NFT collections of monkeys now exist? Also, the CryptoPunk style has been used in many other projects with little success. It works for a little while, but can never surpass the original. You can study and model successful NFT projects, but try to be original. The first of its kind is usually the most successful.

Build a Community

Marketing an NFT is similar to marketing a social media channel or a podcast. Just because you upload a new episode on Spotify or Apple Music each week doesn't mean you will automatically attract new listeners and subscribers. You need to have a creative way to promote your work and build your audience. Who is your typical target avatar? How will you reach your ideal audience? Knowing your audience is essential for your marketing strategy.

But how do you get to know your audience? Simple: talk to your fans. Many artists don't talk to their audience. Find out why they follow you and build from there.

Once you have uploaded a podcast, how are you going to engage people and encourage them to listen to your podcast for the first time? What value are you providing to your subscribers that will make them share your podcast with their friends and come back again for your next episode? What problem are you solving for your audience?

It is great if you already have a long list of existing followers, but they might follow you for plenty of other reasons than your first NFTs. Most likely, they don't even know about NFTs, let alone have an interest in collecting them. That is something to consider as well. You might have to start a process of slowly educating your audience about NFT collecting and why you decided to get into NFTs. You may want to share how you discovered and became interested in NFTs. That way, you are warming up your existing followers to your eventual first NFT drop, and you are slowly creating demand for it.

Most of your audience won't have a digital wallet, yet, or cryptocurrency to buy your NFT. And they won't understand first where the value is in buying and collecting digital assets. Ask if there are people in your audience who know about NFTs and if so, ask them for some guidance. They could give you valuable insight into what it would like to collect from you and then may become your first buyers.

Engage your audience by sharing what you are thinking about doing next and asking for their opinion. That way, you will constantly get valuable feedback and include your audience in your decision making. Depending on the social media platform, the more your audience engages in your posts the higher the algorithms will rank you.

Ask-Me-Anything Session

An ask-me-anything session is very helpful for selling your NFTs. Why? This is when you get the opportunity to tell people about your NFTs. Not only to inform people, but also to gather prospective buyers for your NFTs.

In the session, feel free to answer any questions, because this is when people get to know what your NFTs can do for them and how much they will be worth. Answer all questions thoroughly and be very detailed. This is one of the best strategies out there for achieving a successful NFT sale.

Use Your Email List

Email marketing can help you market your NFTs. How? You can use insightful emails about your NFTs to tell community members about the progress of your NFT journey and any recent updates. Don't worry; big companies do this, too. Doing it in moderation is key to making the most of email marketing. You can use MailChimp to make this process easier.

Promote Your NFTs on Social Media and Online Forums

A major part of your strategy for selling your NFTs is using online platforms. It is not easy and may take a lot of your time, but it is always fruitful. Start sharing something small every day and tell good stories without spamming your followers. Eighty percent should be interesting content without any sales pitch, the rest can be a direct sales post.

Always partake in online forum discussions, especially crypto forums. And when you get substantial attention, it is time to create positive awareness about your NFTs. This way, people will start getting to know what your project is about and, before long, want a piece of it. Some online forums or discussions you can target include:

- Twitter (Twitter is currently the best platform for NFT promotion, there is where most NFT communities are active. Use hashtags like #NFT or #NFTCommunity, which help you to get tracked by like-minded users)
- Discord
- Telegram
- TikTok
- Reddit
- CryptoTalk
- BitcoinTalk
- Instagram

You can also talk to NFT collectors. It is very easy to find them on OpenSea by looking at NFTs similar to what you want to create. You can find the link of the NFT owner and go to their profile on OpenSea where they might have a link to their Twitter account. It won't hurt to send them a message and ask them why they bought certain pieces. Was it because of the aesthetic, investment, or support of the artist? Many of them will be happy to talk to newbies and share their insights. Experiment with several methods of promotion, then pick the ones that work best for you.

Partner with Other NFT Projects

This works too, but more efficiently when you do it strategically. Partnering with like-minded and similar NFT projects allows for cross-promotions, and both sides benefit from doing so. Partnerships don't have to be limited to cryptocurrency and NFTs, you can also test the waters of those worlds. You can partner with popular brands on OpenSea like Coca-Cola, Givenchy, Adidas, and CryptoPunks. Your NFT-based protocol will likely get traction from existing NFT users and brand enthusiasts.

Get Verified on OpenSea

A verified account or collection is marked with a blue checkmark, which helps people to find authentic profiles and collections. OpenSea will usually show a warning message to buyers of NFTs from an unverified collection. This will cause insecurity and prevent many collectors from buying or making an offer. If you have a verified collection, it builds trust for buyers and the standard warning message will not appear when making offers or purchases. We tend to ignore unverified collections when browsing through sales rankings to avoid being scammed, so it's very likely other NFT hunters will ignore your collection if it's unverified, too.

There are two types of verification on OpenSea: Account Verification and Collection Verification, as you can see in the screenshot:

Image 15: Verification badges on OpenSea

To receive a verification badge, your account has either significant interest or sales. Unfortunately, not all accounts on OpenSea are eligible for verification. Here are the criteria you must meet:

- a username, profile picture, and verified email address in your profile
- a connected Twitter account
- your collection needs to have sold at least 75 ETH (or equivalent in SOL) of volume

Once you meet those criteria, you might see a blue banner in your account automatically with a link to apply for verification. Otherwise, you can contact OpenSea to ask for a verification link. If you are a famous public figure, a famous brand, or a famous organization, you have a higher chance of getting verified.

You can lose the verification or never receive one if you engage in deceptive actions on the platform or use copyrighted material or trademarks without a license.

Create a Website

A website is required for everybody who works in the digital world, even if it is just a simple design. You can show off your artwork, link your NFTs to the marketplace listing, and—most importantly—you can ask visitors to subscribe to your newsletter to get informed about your upcoming NFT drops. If you don't have the necessary skills or time to create your website, you can easily hire someone on Fiverr.com to do the work for you.

NFT Roadshow

Successful book authors go on a roadshow before they publish their next book. They schedule radio interviews, TV interviews, and newspaper interviews to promote their latest work. This is the same principle companies apply before they get listed on a stock market. They send out press releases and go around to investment banks and convince them that they are the hottest stock at the moment. Why not organize your own NFT Roadshow in which you explain the number of editions, perks, and pricing? If you get an interview with leading NFT influencers, you have the chance to tell your story and promote your upcoming work. You have to identify which influencers are relevant to your target market, of course. Contact them and ask if they are willing to do an interview with you. Most of them are desperate to deliver new content to their followers.

Optimize Supply

Have you got an idea of how many potential collectors would be willing to spend money on your NFTs? The number of editions that you release, and the price of each item, should align with the maximum number of collectors in your market. Here is where the concept of supply and demand comes into play. The number of editions you drop is your supply. If there is too much supply, people will think your price is overvalued and will not buy. If there is too little supply you will sell it all, but you will lose out on profit because you don't fulfill the demand of your market. However, since you can still collect a royalty on resales, you might want to stay slightly more on the side of lesser supply.

Now you know almost everything that is needed to successfully sell your NFTs. What next? You need to keep the demand up for your NFTs. Do it like nothing else matters. You don't have the time to do all this marketing? Then hire a professional NFT marketing firm who will be in charge of promoting your collections. Go out there and make that money.

It takes time to successfully sell NFTs, but don't be discouraged—this is the way of the future. Get started early and 20 years down the road, your NFTs just might be the key to your early retirement.

Useful Tools for Crypto Artists and NFT Creators

NFT creators need different tools than NFT investors. They need tools that support them in expressing their creativity and the development of such tools is getting better and better. In the following chapter, we will list NFT tools that NFT creators might find useful.

Avoid using free online videos, images, or gif converters of any type, because when you're uploading your creations to the Internet, you never know how their quality may change. Preferably, you use an app or local software on your computer.

NFT Creator	apps.apple.com/us/app/nft-creator/id1562077014

An efficient App for ipads. Import your photos, edit them with filters, graphics and backgrounds. Sell your digital art right from this app.

Sketchar	sketchar.io

Sketchar is an all-in-one mobile app for digital artists to produce and monetize their art, already with a community of 8M+ creators on board.

NFT Art Generator	nft-generator.art

This art generator tool has an easy to use user interface. You can work on your artwork utilizing several layers to create NFT profile images with different traits. Deploy your collections with just one click on the most traded blockchains.

Night Café Creator	creator.nightcafe.studio/create-nft-art

Amazing program to create and organize your artwork. Create NFT Art quickly with the help of AI. Become a crypto artist in minutes without coding, using their bulk creation of NFT art. Harness the power of AI to quickly and easily generate artworks that you can sell as NFTs.

Fotor	www.fotor.com/nft-creator/

Easily create amazing NFT artworks in minutes with the Fotor-NFT Creator. Become a crypto artist with the help of their AI engine. You can apply your images with famous oil painting styles.

Paintstorm Studio	paintstormstudio.com

This is a digital art tool that can produce impressive results. It has a nice Kaleidoscope function and incredible brush settings. A lifetime license is only $19.

VoxEdit	www.voxedit.io

This art generator is specifically for NFTs sold on the Sandbox marketplace. It combines a modeling editor with an animation system and on top you have an NFT maker. When you sell 95% of all transactions goes to you they claim.

Krita	krita.org

Open source drawing program for concept art / texture and matte painters / illustrations and comics that runs on Mac, PC and Linux.

Bomomo	bomomo.com

Simple drawing tool for abstract art with some randomized brush features. It is fun to play around with it for a while.

Lazy	lazy.com

On this platform owned by Mark Cuban you can show your work before launch and. They are still in beta and it seems to us that the development of this site has been stopped.

Courtyard	courtyard.io

Their service is very useful if you already have an existing online shop. They provide an intuitive Web3 checkout that you can drop into your existing e-commerce stack. By integrating Courtyard's customizable solution, you will unlock checkout via all major crypto wallets without writing a line of Web3 code.

Chapter 8: Investing in NFTs (Indirectly)

By now, we hope you have gained a pretty solid understanding of how NFTs work. We know it can feel like diving into a new world with people speaking a different language, and it takes time to feel comfortable in this space. To help you get comfortable faster we offer a very useful "dictionary" on our website (our NFT Insider Glossary) with more than 200 terms and abbreviations used in the NFT space:

www.thevaluebird.com/bonus

When browsing OpenSea, you might also wonder if most of these profile images really are a good long-term investment. To be honest, we don't know.

We believe in the blue chip NFT projects we have listed in chapter 5 because they have proved their concept and we see the progress made in their projects over time. Unfortunately, that doesn't guarantee they will turn into valuable global brands that constantly attract new customers. While some projects become stagnant or even disappear, new trendsetters might gain popularity. Direct investing in NFTs exposes investors to risks that are specific to NFTs and also requires a great deal of knowledge about the NFT market. These two reasons can make it difficult for amateur NFT investors to make the most out of NFT investing. To save time on constant research about new projects, we believe it is also a wise approach to invest in the NFT infrastructure instead of single NFTs. With this method, you can collect profit from the NFT market without risking large amounts directly on a team. This is also in alignment with a wise investment rule: whenever there is a huge gold rush and everyone invests in the gold, you might invest instead in the infrastructure such as the axes, picks, and wheelbarrows to get rich and diversify your portfolio.

We have doubts that some of the extreme prices for single NFTs can ever be achieved again or even topped. Jack Dorsey's expensive first Twitter tweet for $2.9 million could only receive $14,000 in an attempt to re-auction it. The NFT market was in a big bubble in 2021, and it is good that prices have come down in 2022. Prices might go even further down, but we strongly believe in the fundamental technology of NFTs. Single NFT projects might lose their value, but the technology will stay. The European Union announced in September 2022 that they are planning to use NFTs from 2023 to protect intellectual property and fight counterfeits of physical products. In the future, the EUIPO (European Union Intellectual Property Office) might give brand holders the right to issue NFTs that represent digital goods and use blockchain technology to allow an authentic product to be tracked and traced through the entire supply chain.[55] All the luxury brands such as LVMH, Prada, and Cartier are very keen to protect their products from cheap counterfeits.

We've said it before, but we'll say it again: because so few people know about NFTs, now is the time to get involved. Do it before everyone else does. Oh, how we wish we had bought plenty of Apple shares in the year 2000 when the price was $0.20 (price after splitting the share several times). That was before they released the iPod—a device that was totally disruptive to the music industry.

In this chapter, we want to show ideas of the various ways to indirectly invest in NFTs. This is not financial advice— it's purely for educational purposes—but we hope it piques your interest.

Investing in stocks, cryptos, real estate, or NFTs is rarely a straightforward or linear process. You will need a lot of practice and experience before you can get it right. Sometimes, it is good to hold on to an asset during difficult times, and sometimes you gain a lot more if you get in and out at the right time.

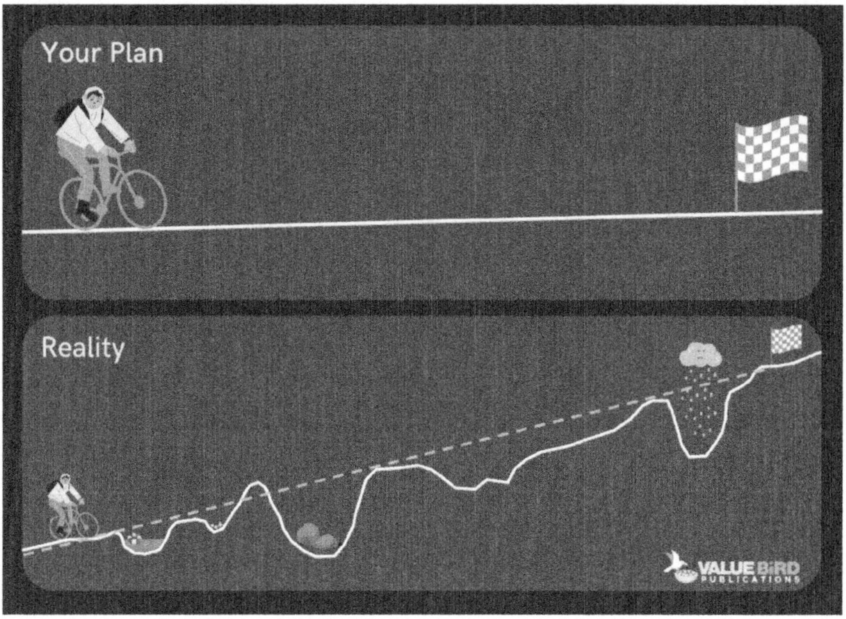

Image 16: Typical investment journey

You might plan for your NFT investment to go without a hitch, but usually, the opposite is true. So, how can you profit from the growing NFT market without investing in them directly? Now that prices are low in both the stock market and the crypto market, the timing might be perfect. Here we have some options:

The Blockchain Technology Used for NFTs

If you want to invest in NFT technology and don't care about the cool artwork, communities, or game utility, the simplest investment strategy is to place some money on projects that develop blockchains suitable for NFTs. You can invest in each blockchain technology by acquiring the cryptocurrency that they issue. Even though NFTs are a completely different universe from cryptocurrency, every NFT blockchain has its native cryptocurrency, for example, the Ethereum blockchain has its currency "ETH," the Solana blockchain has its currency "SOL," Polygon has its token "MATIC," and so on. With the rising popularity of NFTs, it will increase the activity on these blockchains and the demand for its currencies to create, buy, sell, and transfer NFTs.

We will not cover all available blockchains in this chapter but focus on the ones that we see currently as the most important when looking at market capitalization and acceptance on different NFT marketplaces.

Ethereum (ETH)

The most popular crypto for NFT minting, buying, or selling in 2022 is Ethereum. Their cryptocurrency has no limited supply, unlike Bitcoin, but they have a mechanism that reduces the supply of ETH. This could contribute to an increased value added to the many use cases Ethereum has. The current ETH blockchain uses a PoW (Proof of Work) consensus mechanism, but from mid-September 2022, they are going to switch to Ethereum 2.0 using a PoS (Proof of Stake) consensus mechanism. In the beginning, Ethereum didn't have as many users as it has now, which is why it is currently facing unacceptably high gas fees (sometimes up to $800) and long transaction times.

Its Russian co-founder Vitalik Buterin is a celebrity in the crypto scene. He was listed in the Forbes Magazine 30 Under 30 Hall of Fame with an estimated personal fortune of $1.4 billion.[56]

Many analysts see a bright road ahead for this leading altcoin. Some analysts even believe it could overtake Bitcoin because of its open-source technology and many use cases. As you already discovered earlier, Ethereum is the market leader when it comes to NFTs, and it is a prerequisite for creating, buying, and selling NFTs. Instead of spending hours and hours on research about different NFT projects you can just buy ETH, stake it, and profit from each transaction.[57]

Solana (SOL)

Due to Ethereum's high gas fees and low speed, other cryptos like Solana and Polygon gained attention and became long-term rivals for Ethereum. Solana is charging much lower gas fees and is significantly faster than Ethereum using a so-called Proof of History (PoH) consensus. Apart from those advantages, it has created a very interesting ecosystem, even planning to release its own Web3-focused smartphone (which comes with an inbuilt hardware crypto wallet) in the first quarter of 2023. With this smart move, they will step up into the world of Apple and Samsung, reaching maybe a much broader audience outside the crypto scene. They have also opened their first physical store called Solana Spaces at Hudson Yards in Manhattan, NYC in July 2022 where people can set up a wallet, learn about their projects, and purchase T-shirts and merchandise.[58]

Thousands of crypto projects are built on their blockchain, ranging from Web3, DeFi, NFTs, and a lot more. Unfortunately, Solana has experienced several outages, and hackers have attacked the Solana ecosystem and drained around $4 million from Slope wallets.

According to coinmarketcap.com, Solana is number 9 in terms of crypto market capitalization.[59]

Polygon (MATIC)

This blockchain is almost like Ethereum. It is a sidechain (layer 2) of Ethereum (layer 1), which means that it runs on Ethereum. It was developed because of the high gas fees and scalability issues with the Ethereum blockchain. You can call Polygon an addon for Ethereum, which can handle a lot more transactions per second than Ethereum. The transactions are also much faster and cost hardly any gas fees. The higher speed comes from a more centralized technical infrastructure approach—they use only 7 to 10 nodes in their network. It was founded in 2017 by a software company based in India and was originally called "Matic" but got rebranded to Polygon later. The Polygon team is working on a couple of other scalable solutions and has been able to establish important partnerships in the crypto space. According to coinmarketcap.com, Polygon is 12th in terms of crypto market capitalization.[60]

Binance Smart Chain (BNB)

While Ethereum is trying to handle everything, Binance launched their Binance Smart Chain (BSC) parallel to their Binance Chain (BC) to keep up the network speed for both. Their Binance Chain (BC) is being used for sending and receiving digital currencies such as BNB. BNB is their own cryptocurrency, which you can use to pay their gas fees, and it exists on the BC blockchain as a BEP-2 token. For smart contracts, they introduced the Binance Smart Chain (BSC) later in September 2020, and it comes with low gas fees and fast transaction speeds. The BSC uses the BEP-20 standard and is based on Ethereum's source code, which makes it easy for Ethereum DApps to transfer. MetaMask is also supporting BSC tokens. BSC was later rebranded to the BNB chain. And if you are not confused by now, to pay gas fees to deploy or transfer smart contracts on BSC, you need to pay in BNB tokens. You can trade BNB like any other cryptocurrency and also use it in various apps and use cases, including reducing Binance exchange transaction fees and, of course, purchasing, NFTs from their own marketplace.[61]

Binance has a massive user base thanks to its popular crypto exchange and NFT marketplace. They were one of the few companies who still hired new people during the bear market in 2022, while many other companies stopped hiring or even had to lay off their workers (remember, their competitor Coinbase cut 18% of its workforce in preparation for a recession).[62]

Flow (FLOW)

Flow a layer 1 blockchain, developed by Dapper Labs, the creator of CryptoKitties. They were the first to use the ERC-721 standard even before its official release. The CryptoKitties game became so popular that they congested the Ethereum network and therefore Dapper Labs developed their own blockchain, FLOW, to which they switched over in May 2020. Their existing products seem to be mostly used in the sports industry, which include NBA Top Shot, UFC Strike, NFL All Day, LaLiga NFT, the VIV3 NFT Marketplace, and the games CryptoKitties and Cheeze Wizards. We do not see if there is a maximum supply of FLOW on coinmarketcap.com, but FLOW is number 32 in the market capitalization ranking.[63]

Tezos (XTZ)

Tezos was launched in 2018 as an open-source layer 1 blockchain platform. It can also handle smart contracts and it is fast, scalable, energy-efficient, and has low fees. Its native coin is XTZ on the Tezos blockchain. The downside is that currently, only a few NFT marketplaces use Tezos (OneOf, for example).

Chiliz (CHZ)

Chiliz was launched in 2019 as a sports and entertainment blockchain project by socios.com. Their headquarters are based in Malta. The socios.com platform allows users to create and launch fan tokens for sports teams. These fan tokens allow users to participate in the governance and decision-making of the sports team they support. They have secured partnerships with over 150 sports teams in 25 countries. They have also received regulatory approval in Italy.[64]

Originally it was built on Ethereum, but with its high gas fees and slow network, they decided to move away from Ethereum and escape these challenges for their sports community. With its many real-world partnerships, this is a solid project and an interesting investment.[65]

WAX (WAXP)

Wax is considered one of the most energy-efficient networks. Because of its simple nature, it is ideal for NFT minting. You don't have to worry about commission fees when creating your NFTs on their blockchain. Their partnerships include Atari, Funko, Topps, Capcom, and Sony Funimation. The team has an online gaming background and WAX is mostly used in the gaming field. Popular gaming websites could, however, set up a gaming item shop on their website, sell WAX NFTs, and automatically earn commission from every sale. That way, they don't need to rely completely on selling advertisements.

Theta Networks (THETA)

Theta incorporates blockchain with video streaming with the aim of offering a decentralized video-on-demand service, merging it into a single ecosystem on the Theta platform. Theta tokens cannot be mined as all tokens are already in circulation and it is not based on a Proof-of-

Work mechanism.

You can invest in their project by acquiring their Theta Token (THETA), which is used for staking and governance, or Theta Fuel (TFUEL)—the operational token—which is used for gas fees and as rewards for relayers who provide video streams to other users on the Theta network. They seem to be the only blockchain project that focuses on video streaming. As investors, we like when a project has its clear niche. If they can solve the technical problems of video streaming bandwidth and provide a cheaper and decentralized way to stream, this could be the next Netflix.

The Sandbox (SAND)

The Sandbox and Decentraland we described already in chapter 4 (best metaverse projects). A more indirect way to invest in NFTs is by buying virtual land, in which many NFTs will be used, or SAND tokens that are needed to buy and sell NFTs in their metaverse.

Decentraland (MANA)

This has the same approach as Sandbox: the more popular this metaverse becomes, the higher the value of their coin MANA and their virtual land.

NFT-Related Stocks

This is another very interesting way to invest in the NFT infrastructure. Stocks are equity that represent a fraction of ownership of the issuing corporation. Companies can benefit from NFT technology, and if they are listed on a stock market, you can benefit as a shareholder as well. Buying these companies' stock is a great way to jump on the NFT bandwagon without minting your own NFT.

You have to open a brokerage account to purchase these stocks on a stock exchange. Some stocks also pay dividends (usually four times a year), which you will receive automatically in your brokerage account.

Investing in NFT stocks is as risky as investing in NFTs or any other crypto, but to be listed on a stock exchange, companies have to follow strict regulations to prevent fraud and protect investors. Certain key figures of the company have to be transparent and reported regularly, which is not the case with most crypto companies.

Again, this is not financial advice, but here are some stocks that might profit from a growing NFT market:

Coinbase Global Inc. (COIN)

The biggest US crypto exchange got listed on the NASDAQ in April 2021. They opened their own NFT marketplace in May 2022. Coinbase reported a net loss in the first half of 2022 after turning a huge profit in 2021. Users have been staying away from crypto trading as the cryptocurrency markets have been falling lower and lower. The price per stock dropped a lot in 2022, and it might be a good long-term investment to buy at the lowest prices (below $90) because users will come back for trades once the bull market comes back. That Coinbase will survive the crypto winter is very likely since BlackRock, the world's largest asset manager, announced a partnership with them.

eBay Inc. (EBAY)

The world's biggest marketplace for antiques and collectibles acquired the NFT marketplace Know Origin for an undisclosed amount in June 2022. It totally makes sense for them to push into digital collectibles as well. They also announced a partnership with the marketplace OneOf. Once the crypto and stock winter is over, this company might come back to its all-time highs.[66]

Cloudflare Inc. (NET)

They are one of the best global cloud services providers that delivers a range of services to businesses of all sizes and in all geographies. Since all this digital media content has to be stored somewhere, they might profit from the coming NFT boom.

Advanced Micro Devices Inc. (AMD)

AMD is a global semiconductor company whose microchips are used in all kinds of servers, computers, laptops, and other electronic devices. Blockchain algorithms require computing hardware. AMD is researching how to make blockchain transactions faster and more secure. Also, when it comes to blockchain games and metaverses, they will provide their hardware solutions.

Nvidia Corp (NVDA)

Nvidia offers hardware components for the computer, networking, and graphic processing market. Their share already surged nearly 700% when the Bitcoin and crypto mining boom started because there was an increasing demand for GPUs (Graphics Processing Units). Crypto mining companies use Nvidia's GPUs to mine Bitcoins and other digital currencies.

Meta Platforms Inc. (Meta)

Formerly known as the social media corporation Facebook, they have already announced plans to implement a crypto wallet connection to post NFTs on their platforms Facebook and Instagram. They are supposed to support Ethereum, Polygon, and Flow blockchains. It is very likely that their own metaverse will support NFTs as well to be used as avatars, virtual event tickets, and digital fashion.

Matterport (MTTR)

This company's technology is focused on Augmented Reality (AR) and

Virtual Reality (VR) by digitizing, accessing, and managing buildings and places online. Its technology platform uses spatial data collected from a variety of digital capture devices to transform physical buildings and spaces into dimensionally accurate, photorealistic digital twins. It is very likely that their technology will be valuable for future metaverses in which you can visit famous buildings, castles, or museums.

DraftKings Inc. (DKNG)

They are offering platforms for sports betting services, casino games, and fantasy sports. They have launched their own NFT marketplace where you can buy and sell digital sports collectibles. They have partnered with several sports associations such as the NFL, NBA, and UFC.

Funko Inc (FNKO)

Funko is a leading pop culture lifestyle brand. They produce plastic figures, toys, apparel, board games, and recently, also NFTs. They hold a large bunch of licenses and also signed deals with major entertainment companies such as Warner Bros., Disney, and Marvel Entertainment. Part of their business competence is tracking the popularity of a certain item and knowing when to move on to a different character.

Their stock did not suffer very much in the bear market in 2022. In fact, it's up about 30% since the beginning of 2022.[67]

Dolphin Entertainment Inc. (DLPN)

The content production and marketing company teamed up with the crypto exchange platform FTX.US to create an NFT marketplace for sports and entertainment brands.

Hive Blockchain Technologies (HIVE)

This company is mining Bitcoin and Ethereum in cool and politically stable countries (Canada, Sweden, and Iceland) using 100% green energy. They have been listed on the Toronto Venture Exchange since 2017. We are not sure how they utilize all the Ethereum mining hardware after the switch to the proof of stake mechanism, but this company should be watched.[68]

Block, Inc. (SQ)

Formerly known as Square, Inc., this is a company that revolutionized digital payment processing with its point-of-sale software and hardware. They are focusing on small and medium seller businesses providing several solutions such as allowing credit card payments and using tablet computers as payment registers for a point-of-sale system.[69]

Canaan Inc. (CAN)

Canaan Inc. was founded in 2013 and is based in Beijing, China, but they are listed on the NASDAQ. This tech company is working on high-performance computing chip design, chip research and development, and hardware production for Bitcoin mining and artificial intelligence.[70]

NFT ETFs

This is another way you can invest indirectly in NFTs. An exchange-traded fund (ETF) is a type of investment basket that is similar to a mutual fund. Usually, ETFs will represent a particular index, sector, geographic region, or commodity. For example, the ETF SPY represents the S&P 500 index in the USA. They are structured on purpose to follow a certain investment strategy. You can buy ETFs on a stock exchange like a normal stock, and therefore, their prices fluctuate all day as well. You can buy them usually for much lower fees than a mutual fund because an investment manager does not actively manage them. There are also actively managed ETFs, which charge a higher management fee. You can buy an ETF via your brokerage account. There are also monthly saving plans that you can set up in your brokerage or bank account.[71]

Since blockchain technology and NFTs are relatively new, there are few ETF options available. Here are the ones we could identify:

Defiance NFTZ ETF (www.defianceetfs.com/nftz)

Defiance ETF launched NFTZ, an NFT ETF that allows you to invest in NFTs' digital economy, including the NFT marketplaces and the blockchain. The NFTZ ETF is listed on stock exchanges, like the New York Stock Exchange, and is labeled as the first ETF focused on NFTs. If you look at their holdings, you will find many stocks that we already listed above, such as eBay, DraftKings, FNKO, and Coinbase. They will rebalance their holdings on a quarterly basis.

Evolve Metaverse ETF (MESH) (evolveetfs.com/product/mesh)

This ETF, listed on Canada's TSX stock exchange, focuses on the metaverse and virtual reality.

GlobalX Blockchain ETF (BKCH) (www.globalxetfs.com/funds/bkch/)

This is not an ETF that focuses on NFTs particularly, but on companies that are involved in blockchain technology, which as you know by now, is the underlying technology of NFTs. The ETF was formed in mid-2021 and is designed to allow investors to gain exposure to an entire basket of blockchain stocks with a single investment. The annual investment fee is a reasonable 0.50%. The ETF invests in different companies, including several previously mentioned Coinbase, Block, Canaan, and Nvidia. This ETF could be right for you if you believe in the long-term potential of blockchain technology but don't want to guess who will be the winners in the industry.

Chapter 9: Are NFTs a Good Investment? NFT Problems You Need to Know About

A lot has been said about NFTs, from how to buy them to how to create, sell, and even invest in them. By now, you are probably ready to begin your NFT journey or have gone far into it, maybe even making profits already. However, it is wise for you to familiarize yourself with potential problems that may affect your investments. Knowing these problems and how they occur can save you a lot of money. What are these problems, and how can you avoid them? For all the reasons that exist to invest in NFTs, there are reasons not to, and we will discuss that now.

You Can Lose Access to Your Wallet

NFTs are not insured. If you forget the details of your wallet and your seed phrase, you may no longer have access to your NFT. So basically, if you lose the paper on which you wrote down the log-in details or your seed phrase, it is bye-bye to your NFTs.

Unique or Not?

One of the many things that drive people to pay huge amounts for NFTs is the belief that they are holding a unique digital item. This should be expected. After all, scarcity increases the value of commodities. But what happens if the creator of a popular and successful NFT decides to mint more copies of the same content? Of course, the marketplace may block the artist, but the damage has been done, and the NFT you have would drop in value. If it's not unique again, it's not really valuable. How do you guard against this sort of issue? To limit the chances of this happening to you, only buy from blue chip NFT artists or artists you have researched intensively. Established NFT artists can be trusted more because they understand that they risk their professional NFT careers. In general, all transactions are based on trust, so ultimately, you will have to trust the creator of the NFT to keep to the unwritten laws of the trade.

Whistleblower Edward Snowden has criticized crypto and gaming companies for using NFTs to exploit gamers. With NFTs, investors create fake, unnecessary scarcity in a virtual area where there is no scarcity. And virtual metaverses are being used to make huge profits from escapism.[72]

The question here that no one seems to ask is: why do people want to escape from reality and spend more and more time in virtual life? Is our real life not worth living in anymore?

Delivery of Physical Items and Perks

The value of an NFT depends on the various perks it comes with or the access it grants. Some NFTs give the buyer access to a tangible item like an event ticket, the original artwork, or a pair of shoes. But sometimes, the creator of an NFT may renege on their promise to add perks to the token. In this situation, you can report the creator to the marketplace, and they will rightly be blocked or banned, but your money isn't coming back. This is mostly because the blockchain does not recognize tangible items or perks as part of an NFT. Physical items are primarily a marketing technique to increase the customers' desire to buy digital artwork. This tactic negates the trustless transaction that is the major benefit of NFTs. As long as tangible items or perks are involved in an NFT transaction, your only option is to trust the creator of the NFT to be true to his promise. Also, be careful if you buy a hybrid NFT on the secondary market. Once the exclusive T-shirt, pair of shoes, or photo print was redeemed, the NFT might be worthless because the next owner cannot redeem the physical item anymore.

Price Volatility

NFTs increase in value as their popularity grows, and because popularity is a fragile commodity to depend on, the prices of NFTs are very unstable. What could be trending today could depreciate tomorrow. This volatility can also be manipulated with the "pump and dump strategy" by rich colleagues or acquaintances of the NFT creator. They buy all the NFTs, increasing their value and making them popular. After a while, they'll resell it, make their profits, then they'll exit the project.

In addition to the price of your NFT being unpredictable, the cryptocurrency with which all NFT transactions are made is also unstable. For instance, the price of Ethereum fell from a high of $3,939 to $883 in 2022. This provides a great opportunity for sharp investors to purchase more Ethereum to acquire more blue chip NFTs at a low price.

If you are convinced of a project, it is also important to hodl (remember long-term holding?) your NFT even if the prices drop below your purchase price. You never know how much it will be worth in five or ten years. Nevertheless, investing in NFTs is not a safe financial investment and is very speculative.

NFTs Don't Transfer Intellectual Property Automatically

Some NFTs, such as CryptoPunks and CryptoKitties, are structured so that only the original NFT creators can profit from them. They offer you a display license. Bored Ape Yacht Club allows buyers of the NFTs to use them commercially and make profits. In some cases, the NFT contract is drafted to serve as a sort of receipt allowing you to access a digital section of intellectual property, but not the real property. Always check what copyrights you will acquire with your NFT if you plan to use it for commercial purposes.

Lots of Preparatory Steps Before Finding NFT Projects

There are a lot of processes required before one can start trading NFTs. Much of which we've already covered. Remember, even when changing your conventional currency to crypto, you need to get the appropriate crypto wallet for the marketplace you're trading in and have the right cryptocurrency for your NFT. For most NFTs, you will need Ethereum, but for others such as Dronies or DeGods you will need Solana, and you'll need Polygon for Crypto Unicorns and The Martians: Metaverse. For certain crypto tokens, you cannot use MetaMask and will need to get another wallet since MetaMask is mainly for cryptocurrencies based on Ethereum (ERC-20)

Spam

Since some cryptocurrencies such as WAX and Polygon have very low gas fees, there is the danger that people will send you all sorts of spam NFTs. Never click and accept those free NFTs sent to you, because they could contain malicious code that empties your wallet. Hopefully, in the future, this problem will be solved by spam blockers and a function that will burn unsolicited NFTs.

Disadvantages of Blockchain Technology

The decentralized nature of the blockchain makes it a great system. However, it still has its limitations, and you'll face this when you have an issue that requires customer support. You'll discover, unfortunately, that there is basically no customer service system. You have lost your digital asset forever if you mistakenly send a token or coin to a mismatched wallet. No one can help you reverse the transaction or cancel the transfer.

You can suffer significant losses when making a fat finger error. There is a substantial price difference if you transfer 0.5 ETH or 0.05 ETH, so please always doublecheck and never make an offer or transfer in a rush, because every cryptocurrency transfer is irreversible. This is also the reason why plenty of scammers are intent on getting your crypto—they know you cannot reverse any money sent.

In the conventional world, if you order something with your PayPal or credit card and the seller fails to deliver the goods, you can inform the credit card company of the situation. In most cases, you'll be refunded. Additionally, if you lose your card or if your card is stolen, you can message your credit card company to block the card to prevent fraudulent activities.

> *If the seller doesn't ship your online order, you have hardly any chance of getting your cryptos back! Including your NFT. The other person must act and send it to you as a new transfer on the blockchain. Therefore, only do business with reputable and trusted parties when it comes to cryptocurrencies and buying NFTs.*

When it comes to blockchains that have no intermediaries, you are responsible for the actions that you take and the resulting consequences. You are responsible for:

- Determining the trustworthiness of a business partner

- Doing your own research—always!
- Checking correct wallet addresses and compatibility of transfer protocols
- Double-checking the minting websites via social media channels
- Verifying the seller is the content creator or that the owner has bought it from the content creator
- Storing your cryptocurrencies, NFTs, and passwords in a safe location
- Not sharing your private keys with anyone
- Not entering your private keys on a website more than once

Environmental Impact

An increasing number of people view cryptocurrencies and Bitcoins as energy consumers and are therefore wary of investing in such monetary assets. Forbes Magazine recently revealed that Bitcoin consumes the same annual electricity as Norway. But then, the question we should be asking is, what kind of energy is used by Bitcoin miners? Is it renewable energy, energy from fossil fuels, or water-generated energy?

Suppose they're using energy from fossil fuels. In that case, its effect on the environment will be harmful compared to the other two forms of energy generation.[73]

Fortunately, new startups are focused on reducing Bitcoin's carbon footprint and creating new and environmentally friendly ways of mining Bitcoin.

For example, the startup LiquidStack[74] aims to lower the temperature of mining rigs to reduce energy costs. Genesis Mining even exclusively uses clean energy sources.[75]

As mentioned in chapter 1, there are two different ways to conform a block: proof of work (which requires special mining hardware to solve complex mathematical puzzles and therefore demands more electricity) and proof of stake (which requires little computing power, you don't even need special hardware for this anymore). Bitcoin's Proof of Work technology clearly uses substantially higher amounts of energy, but this energy consumption is also what makes Bitcoin so secure and stable for many years.

Another method to reduce computing power and save energy is the pre-mining of all coins that projects such as Ripple (XRP) have used. It works like fiat currency or stocks: a central authority creates a set amount of a cryptocurrency and then slowly releases it into the economy depending on what's going on in the market. This eliminates the need for dedicated high-speed mining equipment (ASIC computers). We do not recommend, for several reasons, investing in Ripple coins, though.

There are already several popular alternative blockchains running that won't put a dent in the environment. They have already been designed to be eco-friendly; for example, FLOW, EOS, and WAX. And in September 2022, Ethereum switched to the Proof of Stake method, which is reducing the network's energy consumption by 99.95%, as they promised.[76]

This upgrade has also reduced Ethereum's insanely high gas fees because since then there will be less computational power required to validate a block.

It is also possible if there is a majority consensus by Bitcoin miners that Bitcoin will switch to a more environmentally friendly method.

Improvement will come automatically since energy prices are rising. Tech leaders are investigating solutions because no serious business owner wants energy costs to eat into the mining profits.

What we miss in the environmental discussion is also the fact that NFTs will reduce paper, plastic, and shipping costs that add to a higher total carbon footprint. We suspect that negative news on Bitcoin's environmental impacts has been circulated on purpose because no one has been complaining about the energy consumption of the traditional banking system—for their virtual and physical transactions, they have servers, ATMs, as well as approximately 600,000 branches in which computers, printers, fax machines, light, automatic door systems, video cameras, alarm, and air-conditioning systems are running. If you add up the energy consumption of all of that plus all the paper they are printing when someone opens an account, the energy consumption is certainly not smaller than Bitcoin's. And no one has questioned their environmental impact.[77]

A 2021 report from Galaxy Digital found that the Bitcoin network consumes less than half the energy consumed by the banking industry. And since Bitcoin is a relatively new technology, improvements and optimizations are inevitable.[78]

Many local authorities are investigating how blockchains can be used to reduce paperwork in accordance with local laws so they can reduce their ecological footprint. For instance, you might be able to visit your town hall in a metaverse in the future.

Avoiding These Scams Will Save You Lots Of $$$

Phishing Emails and Email Scams

You might receive an official-looking email with a link to log in to your bank, crypto, or wallet account. Never ever click a link in any bank account/crypto/NFT related email unless you are 100% certain of its authenticity. Here is an example email from a MetaMask scam:

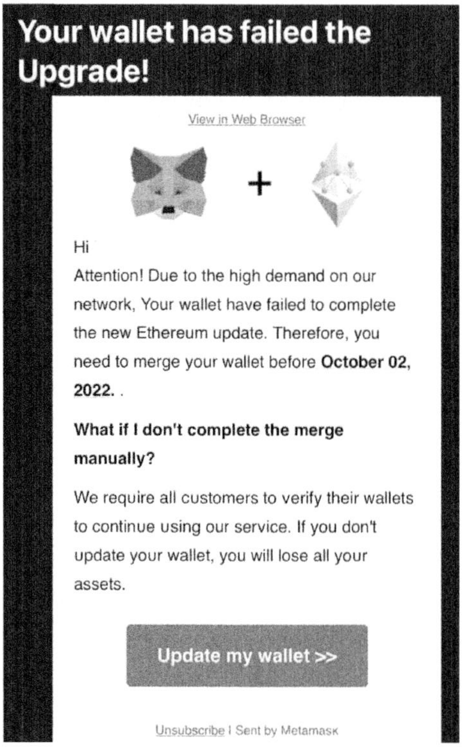

Image 17: Typical MetaMask "Customer Support" scam

MetaMask will never send you an email like this and threaten you with the loss of your assets. They usually don't even have your email address. What could help is to check the sender's email address to see if it really comes from the right top-level domain, and copy the link first into a notepad to see where it leads to. If you have any doubts, call someone at the claimed sender's company and ask if they have sent this email.

Be suspicious about pop-ups as well. Never input your 12-word seed phrase details into a MetaMask pop-up. Actually, never enter your seed phrase again anywhere, and do not share it with anyone and definitely not with any "technical customer support"!

Another popular scam is a message to verify your account for an important minting event. When you click on the link and verify your wallet, they will show an error: *Sorry, something went wrong. Please reinstall your wallet*. And they will ask you to enter your 12 secret words. Never enter your 12 words for these requests. You should only enter them if you start using a new device and you want to use your existing wallet. If you are still unsure if it is a scam, please use a new empty wallet at least, otherwise, you may lose everything you have!

There could even be fake websites pretending to be MetaMask or your wallet's website. Then, you may enter your secret words into that fake website which will allow the scammers to control your wallet. So, always make sure you have your original wallet open.

Discord Scams

The basic principle of Discord scams is usually that a large minting event or bonus sale is happening, and the scammer will inform you about it via a direct message to you. Be aware that 99% of all direct messages are scams. Sometimes the scammers even find your friends and send you a message with the same profile image as your linked friend saying that they have an emergency and if you could send them 0,5 ETH.

Once you join a project server on Discord, go to the privacy settings and disable the direct messages, because scammers' bots will quickly send a message with the same profile logo as the project.

Image 18: Discord Message Settings

In that direct message, they will notify you that minting has now started, and they will provide a link to the minting website. Never click these links in a direct message, always search for the official link in the Discord server channel.

Be extra careful when the minting website shows an error and there is a request to send cryptos in your wallet. Check first in the activity list of your wallet if the previous amount has been successfully sent. Usually, the scammer bots will keep sending you transfer requests, and you might easily click again and again and easily lose easily 1,2,3,4,5 ETH—every click will send money to the scammer.

Also, don't provide your wallet address in Facebook groups where they offer free airdrops for people that post their walled address in a comment. Always search for the official website of the project and check for information. Very often scammers create a similar-looking website with a similar URL, and it is hard to see if it is a fake one.

Safety tip: for minting always use a different wallet address than for your NFT storage. In the MetaMask wallet, you can easily switch between accounts. Rename one account "Minting Only" and "NFT storage" so you can distinguish better between your wallets. That way, if you fall into a minting scam, your NFT collection will still be safe, and you only lose a small minting amount.

Fake Mobile Apps

In addition to fake websites and fake emails, scammers have even created fake mobile apps and inserted them into the Google Play store and Apple App store. Every day, people are falling into this trap of downloading a fake app and transferring cryptos to it just to discover they have lost them all. Apple and Google will remove those apps after a while, but don't hope someone will compensate you for the money you lost. So, always make sure you are downloading the official app of Coinbase, Binance, MetaMask, etc.

Catfishing

These NFT marketplaces claim to be the real deal but are fakes. They could also be impersonators of real and reliable social media sites, celebrities, etc. What they do most is advertise for new NFT collections and drops, which are fake, and might lead to losing all your NFTs or even your money if care is not taken.

Pump-and-Dump Schemes / Rug-Pull Scams

This is especially common for new NFT projects set up by developers. The project has a good-looking website and creates hype that makes the NFTs sell at a very high price. However, once they have sold enough or received money from an investor, they vanish with the funds. Celebrity endorsements and influencers might help ramp up the price, but once it is high enough, they dump the project and disappear.

You can check the buyers of the NFTs on the marketplace. Are they always the same? You may use EtherScan to view all incoming and outgoing transactions. Be careful with collectible projects that ask you to pay a high mint price without a proven track record. They often just want to cash in quick money without long-term interest in the project. For example, Pixelmon minted for 3 ETH and the floor price is now at 0.26 ETH.

Plagiarized NFTs

Yes, it's true, an NFT can't be counterfeited because of the cryptographic signature linked to it. But there are instances where people with ill intent digitize other people's work and turn them into new NFTs. The work then belongs to these scammers, although they are not the original owners of the physical items. Therefore, be cautious if you see a blue chip NFT on some marketplace that costs only 50% of the normal floor price—these are usually illegal copies. OpenSea has faced a lot of backlash recently for allowing users to list stolen or copied NFTs and has promised improvements. However, since they earn 2.5% from each sale, they might have low interest in background checks and verification. This has caused a lot of distress among artists and collectors.[79]

A London-based software company offers a cloning service for your NFTs called CloneMyNFT which allows you to keep an NFT clone in your wallet after you sell your original NFT. It will look identical, but the origin of the NFT is missing. You could even sell this clone if you find a buyer for it. Therefore it is essential to check the authenticity of your NFT carefully before you buy it.

Currency Scam

When you resell your NFT, bidders may change the cryptocurrency utilized without informing you. You may earn 5 DAI (worth $5) instead of 5 ETH (worth between $5000—$20000 depending on the ETH price). Always double-check the currency when buying or selling.

Tinder Scams

This is not a typical NFT scam, but this was a huge crypto scam in 2021. If you are on Tinder and you meet someone who claims they don't work anymore, but live from trading (crypto, gold, stocks, NFTs) and they are willing to show you how you can do the same, run away and block their profile. These people are just trying to scam you by onboarding you on their fake trading platform website.

How to Secure Your Digital Assets: Safety Tips for Your NFTs

Can your NFTs be stolen? Yes, your NFTs are safely secured using the blockchain, but that doesn't mean they can't be stolen. In fact, wallet hacks happen every day, but mostly because their owners fall into a phishing trap or confirm themselves via a random malicious smart contract. Don't worry, we'll give you tips on how to avoid being hacked. For the best safety measures, use cold wallets for your NFTs and practice these tips on how to keep them safe.

Wallet Security

We already explained the different types of wallets in chapter 2 (How to Store Crypto and NFTs Safely). While it is extremely unlikely that the blockchain will be hacked, it is very common to lose your crypto assets in your wallet.

Every wallet is protected by its private key or recovery phrase (usually a sequence of 12 words) which you must never give to someone else or enter on a website unless you want to duplicate your own wallet (a MetaMask wallet, for example) on another computer. Even the customer service of MetaMask and other wallet providers will never ask you for the private key. If someone asks you for it, it is a scam! Don't take pictures or screenshots of your private key, nor store your private key on your mobile phone, a computer, or any other device that has an Internet connection, or in a password manager. Write the words in the exact order on a piece of paper and store it in a safe place, such as in a safe. Laminate the piece of paper and maybe keep a copy in a second safe location. Some people wrote poems with their words, in which every line started or ended with a private keyword. You can also give half of the words to a trusted family member, so only 2 people can restore your wallet access again if you want.

The private keys and the way they are stored are the weakness of cryptocurrency and the blockchain. There is a popular saying:

Not your keys, not your coin.

Be aware that you do not have a private key for any of the cryptocurrency exchanges such as Coinbase and Binance. You log into these exchanges using a normal password. If your exchange disappears, goes bankrupt, or is hacked, you might lose all your cryptos in your exchange account.

As we mentioned already in chapter 4, Coinbase warned their users that they might lose access to their holdings if the company ever went bankrupt, because in the event of a bankruptcy, custodially held crypto assets may be considered the property of a bankruptcy estate. Therefore, to protect your digital assets, never hold large amounts of crypto on a crypto exchange!

To control your cryptos fully, you need to store them on a hardware ledger instead of just holding them on a crypto exchange. Check on your devices periodically to ensure they're not degrading. If they are, transfer your keys to a new storage device.

If you use a MetaMask wallet, we highly recommend not installing it on your smartphone, but only in a desktop browser. If you install it on your smartphone, you have to enter your private key, and this might be backed up when you back up your phone.

Avoid Storing Your NFTs on Exchanges

When you are not currently selling your NFTs (and cyptocurrencies) and you want to keep them until the market value has risen, we recommend storing them in a hardware wallet. Cases have been reported where large exchanges have lost customers' NFTs because of hacks and technical errors. When you are not selling your NFTs, always keep them in your hardware wallet.

Purchase a Hardware Wallet

As mentioned before, a very safe way of storing your digital assets is to use offline crypto hardware wallets. These devices are specifically engineered to store your private keys inside an impenetrable circuit. Never purchase a hardware wallet from Amazon, eBay, or any other online computer shop. The reseller could have tempered the hardware wallet. Always buy directly from the original manufacturer's website. Trusted hardware wallets can be bought from Ledger or Trezor on these websites:

- www.ledger.com
- trezor.io

But don't worry, it is safe to buy our Value Bird paperback, eBooks, and audiobooks on Amazon, they are 100% not hacked—scout's honor—and always deliver valuable content to you. In fact, we at ValueBird would love it if you left us an unbiased review on Amazon. It helps us bring valuable content to more people like yourself.

Use Two-Factor Authentication (2FA)

If you have not activated 2-Factor Authentication for your crypto exchange yet, please go and activate it now. For new accounts it is standard, but old accounts might not have it.

We recommend using an authenticator app such as Google Authenticator (Available for Android and iPhone) which is easy to set up. Keep an export of your google authenticator app accounts in another place, because if you lose your smartphone, you will have trouble getting the random safety codes to log in to your exchanges. The authenticator app does not store any of your passwords. It will randomly generate a PIN every 30 seconds, which you need to enter during the login process.

We used to have text message (SMS) codes for 2FA some years ago, but when traveling, the text messages were not delivered abroad, and therefore it is better to change all accounts with 2-factor authentication to the Google Authenticator app if possible. Also, mobile phone numbers can be spoofed or hijacked (SIM swapping) so that the security code can be requested and received by a hacker. The hacker usually has your personal data and then convinces your mobile carrier to switch your current number to a new sim card. A hacker was sentenced to 10 years in prison for stealing $5 million that way.

Verified Accounts

Be aware that there are many imposters working every day to grab cryptos from newcomers in the NFT scene. They use the same profile image as original accounts and programs, even similar websites so users think they can trust them and will make a purchase. Not all accounts without the blue verified sign are fake, and even verified accounts can be fake if the scammers are smart enough to deceive the marketplace. While the probability is high that a verified account is real, always double the origin is the group or person they claim to be.

Make sure the blue verified sign has a mouse-over message on the blue tick, and also check if the sign is on the right side—if it is on the left, it could be a fake that was included in the logo or text. Here is an example of a verified account on OpenSea:

Image 19:Verified account example on OpenSea

Research Popular Scams

Do your own research to discover which scams are currently running. There are often new scams, and staying up to date will help you avoid them. Read in Discord groups how other people got scammed so you learn from their mistakes. Furthermore, do not 100% trust YouTube influencers. Most of them are paid by projects to push their coin or project, or they push the coins or projects they themselves are invested in. We'll say it one more time: always do your own research.

Use a VPN Service

We highly recommend using a trusted VPN Service while using a public Wi-Fi network. Even in large hotels, you cannot trust Wi-Fi. A colleague of ours was on a business trip in China, and after using the hotel Wi-Fi for one week, he found a malicious software code on the website he was working on. Our email account was hacked, so we had to change our password. Also, you can be directed to any browsing page by Wi-Fi hosts, including fake wallets or crypto exchange sites. Advanced hackers may also collect sensitive details like your password through the network. To be on the safe side, open a secure VPN service channel before you use your wallet. Reliable VPN Services are Express VPN or NordVPN:

- www.expressvpn.com
- www.nordvpn.com

Make a Transfer Test First

As we mentioned earlier, the sender wallet and the receiver wallet must be compatible with the coin or token you want to send. If you try to send 1 ETH to a Bitcoin address, your 1 ETH will be gone. Forever. Therefore, if you want to send a large amount to a new wallet, we recommend sending the smallest allowed amount possible first ($5–$10), to see if it will arrive on the other end. Then send the full amount if that transfer was successful.

Use Complex Passwords

Always use complex passwords when creating a marketplace account or a digital wallet. The longer the password, the better. A combination of lower and uppercase letters, letters, and special characters is less likely to be hacked than passwords containing your birthdate, postcode, or other personal data. Using existing words in your passwords is less secure than a combination that does not exist in a language. To remember your passwords easier, you can use a positive mindset sentence where you only use the first letters of each word, for example,

“**I** am **a** **m**illionaire **u**sing **Bi**nance” and your login password for Binance could be,

$IaamuBi$4438

Avoid writing down your password, as someone might find your notebook. It is also a good memory exercise for your brain to re-create the correct password for each platform.

If you must write it down somewhere, always store it offline on a piece of paper and leave out letters or characters that you know for sure what they are in the password, because you always use the same system. In our example, it could be:

_ _ a a m u B i _ 4 _ _ _

if you always start your password with “**$I**” and finsh with “**438**” then you would know the missing characters, but another person that gains unauthorized access to your notes would still not know the full password. Also, do not expose your full username in that notebook as well, which will also make it more difficult for someone else to use your login credentials.

Use Data Encryption

If you encrypt your data, this will also add additional security to your NFTs and cryptocurrencies. You can download a .dat backup file in your software wallet that contains your keys. Then, encrypt the .dat file using the free, open-source VeraCrypt software and store it on a hard disk or USB device. If a hacker manages to steal the hardware, this encryption makes it harder for them to access your wallet.

Also, use hard drive encryption tools such as BitLocker (free in many Windows versions) to protect your hard disk. If someone steals your laptop, they can remove the hard disk and gain access to all the data on your hard disk. But if you encrypt your hard disk with the BitLocker tool, they will not be able to read the data stored on it because it is encrypted.

Chapter 10: Taxes and Legal Aspects of NFTs

Taxation Aspects of NFTs

We know that the topic of taxes is not the most popular one, and many other NFT books and courses will not talk about it. This is for a good reason because firstly, going through this topic readers start to yawn, and the author won't win a gold medal. Secondly, the authors are not tax advisors and should not give tax or legal advice. Therefore, we also have to give a legal disclaimer: we are not tax consultants and we do not give any tax advice here in this book. Always check with your local tax advisor how to handle profits and losses from your NFT trades, because tax regulations are also different in every country and, in the USA, even in every state.

Since NFTs are a new complex digital asset, not all countries have determined how to tax them. Whether you are a buyer, a seller, or an investor, seek the counsel of your legal or tax advisors when dealing with NFTs. This way, you will avoid errors or omissions when preparing your tax return. To be on the safe side, we assume that they will be handled similarly to cryptocurrencies in your country. In the USA and most other countries, you would have to pay capital gain tax on any profit you make, not on the full amount of your asset. That means each time you sell a stock, cryptocurrency, or NFT you have to calculate the difference between the price it was sold for and the price you paid for the asset including the trading fees, which lower your profits. Any losses and trading fees you can probably offset and therefore it can sometimes make sense to sell a bad asset in your portfolio at the end of your tax year to reduce the taxes you will pay.

In the USA, the IRS taxes cryptocurrencies as property leading to taxable events when you sell crypto or earn crypto dividends from staking. It is similar to stocks. Once you sell crypto, you have to determine your capital gains during the tax year and report them on the correct tax forms. It doesn't matter if you buy and sell ETH for US dollars or other cryptocurrencies such as Bitcoin. In any case, every sale is a taxable event, and you have to determine the cost basis and date of purchase of your initial acquisition and profit or loss at the date of the sale.

If you don't sell, you usually don't need to report your cryptos. But any free airdrops, hard forks, crypto mining income, staking rewards, liquidity pool income, or DeFi interests you will need to report and pay income or capital gain taxes on, or both. Not all tax laws for making profits in the crypto space are clear, for example, many people report it as a mining income, but it is still being discussed whether it should only be taxed when they are sold, not when they are earned.[80]

In some countries, crypto is tax-free if you hold a cryptocurrency for longer than a year, but you still need to document the buying and selling date and price. In the USA, there are cheaper tax rates if you hold your assets for longer than 12 months.

If you trade against Bitcoin, with every purchase or sale of a cryptocurrency, you have to calculate the value in the FIAT currency of your country, such as the US dollar or euro, because the tax authorities only know this currency and not any other.

Donations to charities can also lower your capital gains, and when you take a crypto loan, you can deduct the interest as well. You can also lower the tax you pay by moving to crypto-friendly states in the USA, such as Wyoming, Nevada, and Texas. Internationally, you don't have to pay tax on cryptocurrency gains in El Salvador, Singapore, Portugal, Puerto Rico, Malta, and some other countries. But we wouldn't move to those countries for tax reasons alone because next year politicians might change the tax rules, and then you are back in the same situation. Also, there might be other taxes charged instead, and if you are a business owner in your country, it gets even more difficult to escape the tax authorities. Therefore, always speak to a tax advisor first.

Many people believe they don't need to report any of their cryptos because the tax authorities can't see them. This might be true for past years, but the local authorities are forcing large crypto exchanges to improve their KYC (know your customer) processes in which they verify the identities of wallet owners and store your passport ID. Whenever you exchange cryptos against FIAT or vice versa, your wallet is identified. The European Union is already planning to prohibit anonymous private crypto wallets such as MetaMask in the future.[81] If this becomes reality, future wallet setups will involve giving your personal data to the government and large crypto exchanges will be forced to block transactions to any private, unidentified wallets such as the MetaMask wallet. Also, you never know, it might become mandatory even for software companies to reveal all your transactions from the past years. Therefore, we always recommend documenting your trades and reporting them when you do your tax declaration to avoid being fined or even imprisoned.

For NFTs, the situation is the same. Because they are such a novelty for enthusiasts, people often forget they have to pay taxes on any NFT trade. A long-term investment strategy as mentioned in chapters 4 and 6 is more advisable since there is no tax or lower tax after 12-month hodling (depending on the country you are in).

For NFTs, it is necessary to distinguish between being a creator or an investor.

For creators, any sales from NFTs are seen as ordinary income, even if it is just your hobby. Always check with your local tax advisor, but in general, NFT creators will have to report all the income from NFTs and other sources for each tax year. It should be possible for any fees you pay to be deducted from your NFT income, so always document, not just buying and selling, but also the fees per transaction in dollars or your local currency.

NFT investors have to follow the same rules as are in place for cryptocurrencies, and you have to calculate the gain/loss in your local currency when you sell a digital asset. For example:

NFT bought 12th May 2021	for 1 ETH	= $ 4150
NFT sold 13th July 2022	for 2 ETH	= $ 1050

In Ethereum, you made 1 ETH profit, but for your tax report, you made $ 3100 + gas fees lost (you don't need to exchange your ETH back in US dollars, you just calculate the average daily price in your FIAT currency at the time of the purchase and sale).

Dealing with cryptocurrencies sounds like a lot of work in terms of documentation of each transaction, but don't worry. There are very good tools on the market that will help you to concentrate on your trades and investments and not bury you under a pile of Excel sheets. To our knowledge so far, the best crypto and NFT tax tracking software is cointracking.info. It is very reasonably priced, and there is a free version in which you have to manually enter your transactions, but the pro version is only $11 per month. With the pro version, you can connect to all the popular crypto exchanges via an API interface. Don't panic, an API interface can only read your data, it cannot sell or take your coins on the wallet exchange. API stands for "application programming interface" and it is basically a type of software interface that aids in communication between one or more computer programs.

With our affiliate link, you can get a 10% discount on your account package, and we will receive a bonus as well. We do not recommend this software because of the bonus, but we recommend it because we have used it ourselves for years and it saves us hours of tax work that we would have to do manually otherwise. Our tax advisor is very happy with the automatic reports it produces for our tax declaration, too. You can also connect several online wallets such as MetaMask and Exodus and the hardware wallets Ledger or Trezor. Here is our affiliate link:

cointracking.info?ref=M942815

In our online courses, we will also show you a video on how to configure your API interfaces so all your activities will be logged correctly for your tax report.

You have probably heard of the Bitcoin credit cards that you can use in every shop, just like a normal credit card, but the money you spend is being taken from your Bitcoin wallet. What sounds like a great idea, turns out to be a tax nightmare. Not only will the shop owner have to tediously document the date, time, and the value in FIAT currency of your crypto at the time of purchase, but so do you. We believe many people are not aware of this problem. Unless you live in one of the crypto-heaven countries mentioned above, you have to report to your local tax office every coffee you paid with cryptocurrency, and if the value of your Bitcoin was higher than when you purchase it, you need to pay your personal tax on the capital gain.

We don't know if that was the real reason why Elon Musk ceased to accept Bitcoin as payment for a new car, but there are major tax implications for buyers, too—especially those who invested in Bitcoin early and are now feeling generous when looking in their trading account. They might see a substantial increase in the value of their Bitcoin, but they don't see the amount of tax they have to pay once they sell their holdings. For the IRS in the US or the local tax authorities in your country, spending your Bitcoin isn't all that different from selling it, and therefore makes it subject to capital gains taxes.

If you were lucky and purchased Bitcoins for $1,000 per coin and now use the same coin worth more than $20,000 to pay for your shiny new Tesla, you'll have to report $19,000 capital gains per coin you spend. Did you buy more Bitcoins later for $30,000? Ask your local tax advisor, but later purchases usually do not count. The tax authorities often have the rule, "first in, first out," which means when you sell, the price of your first Bitcoin purchase will be applied.

Please think twice and do your own research if you really want to sign up for one of these crypto-based credit cards. While these cards sound hip and appealing, using them for your weekly shopping will create a tax nightmare, because in most countries, every time you spend cryptocurrency to buy something, you create a taxable event where capital gains taxes must be calculated and paid. And the amount of tax you have to pay then also depends on how long you kept the coin before spending it. However, with a good crypto tax software such as CoinTracking, it might work fine if you link it to your wallet used for your crypto credit card. We have not tried this option yet ourselves.

Legal Regulations of NFTs

As it stands, NFTs and NFT platforms are generally unregulated and operate freely, allowing transactions that would not be permitted in other financial markets. Sellers on those marketplaces are not required to go through any "know your customer" process before they are allowed to make a sale as they would be on traditional Internet platforms. The absence of laws surrounding the use and trading of NFTs presents some problems and risks. Since blockchain technology and smart contracts are still relatively new, there are no specific laws targeting the use of NFTs. This kind of unclear situation leads to possible several legal issues with NFTs.

> *All information in this chapter and book is not intended as legal advice. The information presented here is merely to increase the reader's awareness of possible legal issues. Only accept legal counsel from a lawyer.*

Are NFTs Securities?

A security is a financial instrument used to raise capital in public or private markets that can be traded, for example, stocks, bonds, options, futures, and banknotes. All securities are fungible, meaning interchangeable. Your 100 shares of AMD are just as good as my 100 shares of AMD. Why does it matter if NFTs or cryptocurrencies are securities? It matters because if they are securities, they must fulfill strict rules and regulations to protect investors from being defrauded. In the US, the SEC (Securities and Exchange Commission) is responsible for all security regulations.

To know whether a cryptocurrency or NFT is a security or not, it has to pass the "Howey test." This test finds its origins in a Supreme Court case in 1946, in which the Howey Company was selling tracts of citrus groves in Florida to residents, then leasing it back to the company to grow and sell citrus fruits and shared the profit with the new landowners. The SEC intervened claiming this kind of arrangement is an investment contract and thus a security that requires SEC registration. In a landmark decision, the Supreme Court defined four criteria for determining whether an investment is a security. This became the so-called "Howey test." The four requirements are:

1. An investment of money
2. In a common enterprise
3. With the expectation of profit
4. The profit is being derived from the efforts of others[82]

In the case of the Howey Company, the buyers of the citrus groves considered the transaction valuable because the labor and expertise were provided by others. The buyers only needed to invest capital to gain an income stream. This classified the transaction as a security (or investment contract) that must be registered with the SEC.

Since Bitcoin and other cryptocurrencies are decentralized, they are difficult to regulate. In 2018, the SEC declared Bitcoin not a security because it is a replacement for the dollar, the euro, or yen and there is no central company controlling it. Most altcoins, however, are most likely to be considered securities since they often have a central enterprise controlling them. Since 2020, the SEC has been suing Ripple Labs, claiming the XRP token is an unregistered security and tokens used in ICOs (initial coin offerings) are all considered securities. Startup companies often use crypto tokens as a means of funding through ICO. Furthermore, the SEC has been targeting crypto lending products in recent years.

The SEC is still analyzing how NFTs fit within present-day financial regulations. Are NFTs securities? NFT fans would prefer to avoid the complicated process of registering the tokens, of course. SEC investigators have taken a particularly keen interest in fractional NFTs in which shares of the split token can be bought and sold. The key distinction between NFTs and cryptocurrencies is, of course, their lack of fungibility.

Fungibility is an extremely useful quality in a security and a precondition to a liquid secondary market. But nonfungibility is not a necessary characteristic of a security. And fungibility is not an element of the Howey test. Therefore, NFTs must have something other than nonfungibility to not be considered a security by the SEC. This is because an investor who purchases an NFT is making a monetary investment with a reasonable expectation of profits. The question for NFTs is whether the profit is derived from the efforts of others in the future. If no future third-party efforts are needed to realize an NFT profit, the item is no more a security than a painting hung on a museum's wall. Viewed through this lens, we can assume that Beeple's *Everydays* NFT is not a security. The work of art when it was sold at Christie's exists in its final state, and even if Winkelmann never creates another artwork, this particular NFT has scarcity value and, for some, aesthetic appeal.

Of course, many art collectors will make a purchase with the hope that the work will rise in value as the artist becomes more famous. But from a Howey test perspective, this type of appreciation is not due to the efforts of others. It is too unclear who the "others" are. Is it a crowd of critics, gallerists, museums, or famous collectors?

However, some NFTs may well have value added that depends on the Howey-like efforts of others.

If you are creating and selling your own NFT, we advise you to speak to a lawyer. Try to market them as products, art, or collectibles, and avoid labeling your digital asset "a good investment," which would be a surefire way to invite regulatory scrutiny. Also, avoid contract terms stating that you will get a share each time your NFT is sold again. Such stipulations are becoming more common among artists, as they desire to generate passive income from their NFT sales, but they're also attracting SEC attention, implying expected profits in the future. Unfortunately, resale rights are not recognized by the law, and NFT creators will have no way of addressing possible losses and claiming their royalties.[83]

There are also issues that relate to using NFTs as a way to raise money for a business (including DAOs) or that pay royalties to those who purchase them. If royalties are being paid out, that could be considered ongoing profits from the effort of others. Navigating this space can be tricky since NFTs have implications in a variety of areas, ranging from securities law to intellectual property concerns to contract law.

Apart from NFT sellers who have to be concerned about security regulations, the NFT marketplaces should be concerned as well. If a marketplace provides securities, it must register with the SEC and comply with its regulations.

Intellectual Property and Copyright of NFTs

Intellectual property rights play an important role in the art world and with NFTs as well. They refer to creations of the mind, such as inventions, literature, art, designs, names, and images.[84] It covers the following types:

- Copyright
- Patents
- Trademarks
- Industrial designs
- Geographical indications
- Trade secrets

Let's look at copyrights, which are most relevant for NFTs.

Copyright is the right of the original creator to make copies for a specified time period. Copyright comes once the work is finished in a tangible medium; therefore brand names, logos, and domain names cannot be protected under copyright law. The work has to be written down, drawn on a canvas, or saved into a hard drive. Very important: when you purchase any form of art (including an NFT) you are NOT acquiring the copyright. The creator will keep the copyright unless there is a written statement of the creator to permit full or partial copyrights to you. If nothing is mentioned in the description of the NFT, you only have the right to use and display it for personal, but not commercial, purposes. You are not allowed to sell more copies of the NFT content or make derivative works. Therefore, be careful regarding what you want to do with your NFTs and check the details before you buy one if you plan to monetize the artwork.

If you are creating NFTs, it is always best to create an original work of art or design. Do not grab any images, videos, or music off the Internet for making new NFTs because these items are most likely protected by copyright. Ask the copyright owner beforehand if you can get a license to use the piece. You might have to pay the license upfront, and it is usually only valid for a limited time period and in a certain geographical region. For NFTs, you need a worldwide usage license, of course.

If you hire someone to do the artwork for your NFT, make sure you have a written agreement that declares that you own the copyright of the work. In your contract, mention the term "work for hire" which makes it clear that you will have the copyright delivered with the work. This is why it is important to research and seek legal advice to better understand the laws guiding the NFT creating or purchasing process.

Once an artwork is no longer protected by copyright, it falls into the so-called "public domain." Once a work is in the public domain, you can use it freely without having to ask the owner for a license. You can even sell public domain art as it is. But when you mint an NFT, it must be your original work. You should never mint a public domain artwork (unless you're using only some parts of it). Unfortunately, it takes many years until the copyright expires and the object becomes public domain, depending on the country you are in, it may take 50, 70, or even 95 years.

In a major change for a popular NFT project, Kevin Rose, founder of Moonbirds, announced on Twitter that both Moonbirds and Oddities will move to a CC0 license. CC0, otherwise known as Creative Commons, simply means "no rights reserved" on intellectual property. It's a form of copyright that allows creators to waive legal interest in their work and move it into the public domain. This means that anyone can now use Moonbirds NFT art freely without any copyright restrictions. Of course, not all Moonbirds holders were happy about that decision, and the floor price dropped drastically. However, in the future, the price might rise again because everyone can now use a Moonbirds and stamp it all over any type of merchandise, from coffee mugs to baseball caps. This could make them more famous than they currently are, and the demand might increase again.

If you are planning to use an image of someone famous, there might be some legal issues associated with that. Even if you take a photo of a celebrity, that celebrity might have rights to your photo.

Conclusion

Are NFTs a good investment? It's difficult to say. After reading this book, you now know the advantages, risks, and problems of NFTs. But if we think about the long-term perspective, nobody really knows where NFTs will go. Serial entrepreneur and bestselling author Gary Vee said 98% of NFTs will go to zero. Being the CEO of his advertising agency, he is considered one of the leading global minds on what's next in culture, relevance, and the Internet. He is expecting a giant crash in the NFT market. Why? Because the NFT market was extremely hyped up and oversaturated in the few last years; it resembles the 1990s tech boom from which only a few survived.[85] The question is if we have already reached the bottom in 2022 or not.

Of course, many NFTs are creations with no utility, but if you pick the right ones, we highly believe they can be an interesting diversification to your investment portfolio. Don't let the negative parts discourage you, because if you don't diversify your investments, it could present an even bigger risk. NFTs aren't without their problems, but as they become more mainstream, with evolving technology and consistent new upgrades, NFTs can overcome some of the technical barriers and disadvantages they currently have. We cannot ignore the fact that they do have space to grow in the future and they will be expanding to new areas.

From an investor's perspective, NFTs open up a whole new asset class, and thus enormous opportunities. This is especially true if you are an artist—they could lead you to an entirely new audience. To sell NFT art successfully, you need to have a concept, a story, and a good social media following. This can come in many forms, such as, for example, Benyamin Ahmed, the 12-year-old programmer creating pixel art, and his Weird Whales collection.

Our advice is not to rush in quickly. Research NFT projects, start observing the market, follow NFT news, and look for upcoming projects that have a lot of potential. Remember, non-fungible tokens are still in the beginning stages, which means they have the potential to expand beyond digital images, music, and videos. You are still an early bird because 90% of the population does not yet know what NFTs are. But this can change fast when Twitter, Instagram, TikTok, and Facebook implement them in a user-friendly way into their social media platforms.

Ethereum was already running four years ago, but many people were unaware of it. Now, it seems it could become more important than Bitcoin itself with its many use cases from DeFi, NFT minting, and being the technical foundation of various altcoins.

Non-fungible tokens will have a bright future for sure, not just because art goes more digital, but also because the whole world is in the process of being digitized. Just look at what Google maps has done: they have mapped out nearly the whole world. Since the main benefit of NFTs is the proof of ownership, it will lead to the NFT-ification of everything that makes sense in the next decade. NFTs will also play an important role in future metaverses as in-metaverse items. The metaverse will be the next evolution of the Internet and social media. The future of NFTs is being created while you are reading these words, and now you know how to join in.

We hope you enjoyed reading this book. We would appreciate it and be incredibly grateful if you could leave a positive review for this book on the platform where you bought it.

☆ ☆ ☆ ☆ ☆

Many readers are unaware of how important it is for independent publishers to have reviews and how difficult it is to gather them. Reviews really help us tremendously to get in front of the right audience and help more people to gain financial education.

Do you want to receive more relevant NFT and financial news from the Value Bird? Download our free gifts and subscribe to our insider newsletter on:

www.thevaluebird.com/bonus

Alternatively, follow us on Twitter (**www.twitter.com/TheValueBird**) or Telegram (**t.me/valuebirdnft**)

We would like to hear from you and wish you good luck on your NFT journey.

NFT Insider Glossary

At the beginning of our NFT journey, we did not understand very much what was written and discussed, and we believe you will be just as confused as we were when you dive into NFTs. It is as if people speak a different language.

To help you feel comfortable much faster in the NFT world, we will now let you in on the insider language of the NFT communities. We have done the work for you and collected words, terms, and acronyms that you might stumble over when joining Discord groups or following NFT artists on Twitter.

#

1:1
pronounced "one of one" is a unique, single edition NFT, as opposed to an NFT that's part of a multi-edition collection

10K PROJECT
A collection of 10,000 NFTs.

2FA (TWO-FACTOR AUTHENTICATION)
a second form of authentication during the login process, additional to your password, to protect your account on a platform from being hacked.

51% ATTACK
an attack on a blockchain made possible when a single person or group gains control of over 50 % of a blockchain's hashing power, enabling them to block new transactions from being confirmed as well as change the ordering of new transactions. It also allows users to rewrite parts of the blockchain and reverse their own transactions.

$
a dollar sign at the beginning of a ticker code indicates that this is a cryptocurrency, example $ETH

A

AB
Art blocks, a marketplace for (generative) NFT art

AFAIK
As Far As I Know

AIRDROP
A distribution of a cryptocurrency token or an asset like an NFT, usually for free, to numerous wallet addresses as part of a marketing campaign in order to gain attention and new followers. Can be a trick used by scammers to send fake tokens to your wallet that then empties your wallet when you connect to it to the scammers website.

ALGORITHMIC STABLECOIN

A stablecoin that maintains its target price by implementing various market incentives and mint / burn techniques, while an asset-backed stablecoins, which maintain reserves of US$ or other assets to back their value.

ALPHA

someone shares information that gives you an advantage in a valuable investment

ALTCOIN

Any cryptocurrency that isn't bitcoin (alternative coin)

AMA / ASK ME ANYTHING

is a specially session commonly used among NFT creators in online communities, usually on Discord.

AML (ANTI-MONEY LAUNDERING LAWS)

laws, regulations, and procedures aimed at uncovering efforts to disguise illicit funds as legitimate income.

ANON

Anonymous. People who are online using a nickname rather than their real name.

APING / APE IN / APED

to buy into a cryptocurrency or NFT in the hope it will skyrocket like the Bored Ape Yacht Club, usually out of FOMO. Also investing large amounts of cryptos without any background knowledge.

APY (ANNUAL PERCENTAGE YIELD)

rate of return on an investment, including the effect of compounding interest. This has nothing to do with HARDWARE WALLETS which store your Bitcoins once they were mined.

ART REVEAL

After a period of waiting, an exciting moment in an NFT collection launch. Holders of the NFT and the general public can finally see the specific artwork they've minted. Often used as pre-mint teasers to generate interest around a project.

ASIC (APPLICATION SPECIFIC INTEGRATED CIRCUIT)

a computer designed for mining proof of work cryptocurrency such as BITCOIN

ATH

All-Time High price of a cryptocurrency, stock or NFT

ATM

at the moment

B **BA**

Bored Ape

BAGS

NFTs that someone owns, as in "my AB bags" – my Art Blocks NFTs

BAYC
Bored Ape Yacht Club, see chapter 4 of The Ultimate NFT Guide book
BEP2
Binance chain standard token
BEP20
Binance smart chain token
BEAR MARKET
prices in a market will go down in a bear market – opposite of BULL MARKET
BLOCKCHAIN BRIDGE
allows the transfer of data between two different blockchains
BLOCKCHAIN EXPLORER
a website to search and browse blockchain records
BRB
Be Right Back
BRO
brother / friend
BTC
this is an abbreviation and exchange symbol for "Bitcoin"
BTM
a cashpoint (ATM) that allows users to buy and sell BITCOIN
BULL MARKET
prices in a market will rise and rise – opposite of BEAR MARKET
BURNING / BURNED
a process to remove tokens from circulation in order to increase value due to less availability. The process of burning involves sending the token to a wallet address that is unable to send tokens, permanently locking it there.

C **CASH GRAB**
Projects that are only about making a quick profit that will disappear with the money, often celebrities NFTs who have never been previously been active in the NFT world.
CBDC (CENTRAL BANK DIGITAL CURRENCY)
Most central banks of each country plan to replace all FIAT cash sooner or later with a new digital cash version to better control and monitor where, when and on what you are spending your money. This will lead to the complete loss of personal anonymity and freedom of humanity.
CC0 (Creative Commons Zero)
the most liberal form of copyright protection in which creators allow the public to use, adapt, or profit off of their work (no rights reserved).
CENTRALIZED EXCHANGE (CEX)
A cryptocurrency exchange owned by a centralized entity.
CMB / CYB
Count My Blessings / Count Your Blessings

COLD WALLET / STORAGE
a cryptocurrency wallet that is not offline (not Internet-connected), in contrast to a "hot wallet" – see chapter 2 of The Ultimate NFT Guide book

CP
CryptoPunk

CUSTODIAL
Crypto businesses that hold customer's digital assets and you will not have the private keys

DAO / DECENTRALIZED AUTONOMOUS ORGANIZATION
an organization represented by rules encoded as a computer program that is transparent, only controlled by members of the organization and not influenced by a government.

DAPPS / DECENTRALIZED APP
an app that runs on decentralized networks

DED
dead, as in worthless

DEFI / DECENTRALIZED FINANCE
a blockchain based form of finance using smart contracts that does not rely on central financial intermediaries such as brokerages, banks or exchanges, for example loan platforms, insurance providers, investment and savings accounts.

DEGEN
degenerate

DEX
Decentralized Exchanges that allow peer-to-peer transactions rather than going through a third party, for example Uniswap or SushiSwap

DECENTRALIZED SOCIAL MEDIA
social media platform that is based on blockchain

DERIVATIVES
in the NFT world an imitation project, for example other NFT collection displaying monkeys.

DGAF
Don't Give A Fuck

DIAMOND HANDS
someone who holds their cryptocurrency or NFT until they reach new ATHs.

DISCORD
instant messaging platform for voice, text, images and video. Users can either communicate in private messages or in more public communities called "servers." Each server can contain a number of chat rooms. To access these servers, you need an invitation link. Discord has become the primary medium for communication for many NFT communities.

DOPE
something very cool, as in "this is dope!"

DOUBLE SPENDING
a possible flaw in a digital cash scheme in which the same single digital token can be spent more than once.

DOXXED
someone who is not anonymous, for example the developers behind a project. It's less likely a project will be a scam if team members can be traced.

DROP
This is an event where users receive free tokens for holding onto certain types of assets / cryptos, also see AIRDROP

DYOR
Do Your Own Research

E **ETH**
This is an abbreviation for Ethereum, which is the second biggest cryptocurrency after bitcoin (BTC). It is a popular blockchain to store NFTs, Dapps and smart contracts.

ETH2.0
the upgrade in September 2022 to the Ethereum network that changed the PoW consensus mechanism to PoS to improve scalability and lower energy consumption.

ERC-20 (Ethereum Request for Comment - 20)
standard for fungible tokens for the Ethereum network

ERC 721 (Ethereum Request for Comment - 721)
standard for non-fungible tokens for the Ethereum network

ETHERSCAN
This is a BLOCKCHAIN EXPLORER to check transactions and purchase price of digital collectibles.

F **FACEMELT**
when prices increase drastically

FCFS
First Come First Served, often used for NFT collection drops

FIAT
This is a name for government-issued currencies like USD, EURO and GBP.

FLOOR PRICE
The floor price of an NFT collection is the lowest listed price in the entire collection. The value of a collection is often dictated by this price.

FLOOR SWEEP
is to buy the cheapest NFT(s) in a collection.

FOMO
This stands for "fear of missing out". This fear arises in people when they see a fast increase of the price and they are not invested in this item.
FORK
creating a new version of an existing blockchain or project. Often done to start a new project that is similar to an existing one, to take advantage of the work that's already been done.
FR
For Real? In the meaning of "Is it true?"
FREN / FRENS
friend / friends
FRACTIONAL OWNERSHIP
Partial ownership rights over an NFT. Sellers can sell percentages of a work and buyers can buy what they can afford.
G **GAS**
An amount required to perform a blockchain transaction on the blockchain. You have to pay gas fees every time you buy an asset, send ETH to a different wallet or set up a smart contract. Gas fees usually compensate blockchain miners for the computing power they have to use to verify blockchain transactions. The price fluctuates based on network congestion - the more people using the network, the higher the gas fee.
GENESIS PIECE
the first piece of work of an artist
GG
Good Game, as in "This is a gg."
GM
Good Morning – a typical start of a tweet or conversation.
GMI
Going to Make It. To motivate other members of the crypto-community. Opposite of NGMI
GN
Good Night
GOAT
Greatest Of All Time, for example ETH is the GOAT! Also expressed via a goat emoji.
GOVERNANCE TOKEN
a token that represent a person's stake in the governance of a project, usually granting them voting powers.
GTD
Going To Dust. Used when a coin or NFT looks like it was a bad investment.
GTFO
Get The Fuck Out (of this coin or NFT)

GWEI
One billionth of an Ether (ETH) also known as a Nanoether, the unit used to price Ethereum gas transactions.

H **HARD FORK**
is a radical software upgrade of a blockchain that requires all validators in a network to upgrade to a newer version. It could make previous transactions and blocks invalid and it's not backward-compatible as a SOFT FORK would be.

HARDWARE WALLET
a type of cold wallet (offline wallet) where cryptocurrency is stored on a physical device much like a flash drive (but often with security features).

HFSP
Have Fun Staying Poor. Often the answer to someone who doesn't understand crypto or NFTs and doesn't want to invest in it.

HMU
Hit Me Up / get in touch with me

HODL
This means to "hold on" to a coin even in times of dropping prices.

HODLERS
Crypto slang for a person holding their assets over the long term.

HOT WALLET
A cryptocurrency wallet that has internet connection, which allows the currency to be quickly accessed for trading and transactions.

HW
can mean hardware wallet such as Trezor or hardware (depends on the context)

I **ICO (INITIAL COIN OFFERING)**
a new coin is being bought at the first stage before it goes to an exchange for the public. Prices rise at the exchange mostly, because of the hype that is being created when a coin is being released. Equivalent to an IPO (= initial public offering) on a traditional stock exchange.

IDK
I Don't Know.

IDEK
I Don't Even Know.

IDGAF
I Don't Give A Fuck.

IPFS (INTERPLANETARY FILE SYSTEM)
A peer-to-peer network or protocol using a decentralized file system to store and distribute data.

IMO
In My Opinion

IRL
In Real Life - outside of the online/virtual world.

J **JFC**
Jesus fucking Christ

K **KMS**
Kill MySelf

KYC (KNOW YOUR CUSTOMER)
a procedure to verify the identity of a customer. In the crypto world this means to identify a person behind a cryptocurrency wallet or a user of a crypto exchange.

L **LAYER 1**
is the base blockchain, for example Ethereum and Bitcoin. It is the underlying foundation that various layer 2 networks build on top of.

LAYER 2
projects that build projects on for example Ethereum and the lighting network on top of bitcoin. Layer 2 will help to reduce gas prices and make faster transactions.

LFG!
Let's Fucking Go! Used to express when in two minds about a risky NFT trade.

LMAO
Laughing My Ass Off

LMFAO
Laughing My Fucking Ass Off

LMK
Let Me Know

M **MARKET CAPITALIZATION**
the total value of all coins that have been mined of a cryptocurrency. Often higher than the value that could be realized if the majority of holders of a currency decided to try to cash out.

MAINNET
is an independent blockchain with its own protocols

MAXI / MAXIMALIST
a person who holds extreme views on a particular cryptocurrency, typically a Bitcoin Maximalist

MEMECOIN
Cryptocurrency that originated from a meme or has some humorous character, for example Dodgecoin or Shiba Inu.

MEATSPACE / MEATVERSE
opposite of the metaverse: the real life

METAMASK
is an online digital wallet for the Ethereum standard.

METAVERSE
a virtual reality world where people can interact. Many NFTs may be used in future metaverses. Also see our free metaverse guide on www.thevaluebird.com

MFER
"motherfucker"

MINERS
Contributors to the validation of transactions of a blockchain.

MINING POOL
the pooling of resources by miners, who share their processing power over a network and they split the reward equally.

MINTING
the process of creating new tokens on a blockchain, often related to NFTs.

MM
see METAMASK

MOBILE WALLET
mobile phone software (app) for the storage of cryptocurrency.

MOON/MOONING
when a coin or token goes exponentially up in price ("to the moon!")

MVP (MINIMUM VIABLE PRODUCT)
"is a version of a product with just enough features to be usable by early customers who can then provide feedback for future product development."[1]

N **NEW COINER**
someone new to the cryptocurrency space.

NFA
Not Financial Advice

NGMI
Not Going to Make It

NMP
Not My Problem

Nocoiner
someone who holds no crypto coins and believes they are scams or pyramide schemes, usually a NORMIE.

NODE
is a redistribution point of the data on a blockchain

NOOB/N00B
someone not experienced in cryptos or NFTs and can easily fall for scams such as pump and dump schemes.

NORMIE/NORMY
a person with a regular, conservative lifestyle, for example, has a 9–5 job, a mortage, is married and live in the suburbs.

O **OFF-CHAIN**

when something is not store on the blockchain itself, for example, the image or video file of an NFT.

OG

Original Gangster, meaning a first in its space project such as CryptoPunks. Someone who has been around since the beginning of NFTs or cryptocurrencies. Getting in on a OG project before prices start to explore and before the project is considered OG is like winning the lottery.

ON-CHAIN

anything that is store on the blockchain.

P **PAPER HANDS**

someone who sells their digital assets at the first hint of a market downturn, usually for a price less than purchased.

P2E (PLAY-TO-EARN)

an online game in which players are rewarded with cryptocurrency tokens or other blockchain-based items, which can be converted into other crypto or fiat currencies.

P2P (PEER-TO-PEER)

this means between you and me, without any intermediary.

PEGGED CURRENCY

A STABLECOIN PEGGED TO A FIAT CURRENCY

PFP (ProFile Picture)

NFTs used on social media, for example Bored Ape Yacht Club, Cryptopunks or Doodles.

POAP NFT (PROOF OF ATTENDANCE PROTOCOL NFT)

an NFT awarded to attendees of events as a proof you attended.

POS (PROOF OF STAKE)

a mechanism for blockchains that work by selecting validators in proportion to their quantity of holdings in the associated cryptocurrency. Avalanche, Cardano, Ethereum (since September 2022), Polkadot, Solana and Tezos are POS blockchains.

POSITION

when you buy a cryptocurrency or token you take a position in expectation the price will go up. A short position means you have sold a cryptocurrency or token in expectation of closing your trade with profit at a lower price.

POW (PROOF OF WORK)

a mechanism for blockchains in which one party (the prover) proves to others (the verifiers) that a certain amount of a specific computational effort has been expended. Bitcoin and Monero are POW blockchains.

PPL

People

PRIMARY MARKET

Market determined by the initial sale of an asset. See also SECONDARY MARKET

PRIVACY COIN

Cryptocurrency that preserve anonymity by obscuring the flow of money across their networks, for example MONERO coin.

PRIVATE KEY

a piece of code, that grants you the ownership of the crypto funds on a certain cryptocurrency address. It pairs with a PUBLIC KEY. You must never ever share your private key with anyone.

PROBABLY NOTHING

Used ironically, meaning it is probably something important.

PROPS!

Proper respect! An expression of admiration.

PUBLIC KEY

a series of numbers, letters and symbols to encrypt information

PUMPING AND DUMPING

a group of investors that artificially inflating the price of a token or coin with false information, allowing those behind it or who got in early to then sell off and cash out before the price drops too much.

R **RECOVERY SEED/PHRASE**

a list of 12-14 random words used as a backup for your crypto PRIVATE KEYS. You must never ever share your private key with anyone.

REKT

slang for wrecked (usually for trading losses)

RIGHT-CLICKER

a pejorative term for people who are skeptical of NFTs. It originates from the idea that instead of paying for digital art you could simply right-click with your mouse and save the file to the computer.

ROADMAP

A document that maps out the goals and next steps for an NFT project.

ROYALTY

a specific price paid for owning, creating, or licensing a work. Many NFT creators receive a predetermined percentage of the sale price every time their work is sold on an NFT marketplace, making money from every transaction.

RN

Right Now. As in "Sell it RN!"

RUG PULL / RUGGED

when a development team suddenly abandons a project and takes all the money out and you are REKT. Also used in "It's a rug" or "getting rugged".

S **SATS (SATOSHIS)**

smallest denomination of a Bitcoin. Satoshi Nakamoto is the name of the inventor and creator of the Bitcoin whitepaper. It is unknown if Satoshi is a single person or group of people as their identity has never been verified.

SCAMMER

someone trying to steal your crypto or NFTs. The lowest form of life.

SEC (SECURITIES AND EXCHANGE COMMISSION)

is an independent agency of the United States federal government that enforces the law against market manipulation in order to protect investors and maintain fair markets.

SECONDARY MARKET

Market determined by sales after the initial sale on the PRIMARY MARKET.

SEEMS LEGIT

a common expression for a promising project, but could also be used ironically

SEEMS RARE

a common, sarcastically reply to a NOOBSs question when asking for feedback on their NFT.

SER

wrong spelling for "Sir"

SHARD CHAIN

a sub-blockchain of a main blockchain network operating independently to facilitates transactions. Transactions are still secured by the main blockchain. Primary purpose is to help process transactions faster and easing the blockchain network's congestion problems.

SHILLING

Shilling is spreading propaganda enthusiastically to promote something for a financial incentive. It's not illegal, but it is a form of spam to manipulate prices. The expression "No shill!" could therefore mean "I'm not trying to push this project out of self-interest!"

SHITCOIN

a coin having no real potential value or usecase. Some people, called Bitcoin MAXIMALIST, anything other than bitcoin is a shitcoin (also known as an altcoin).

SIDECHAIN

a secondary blockchain that is connected via a bridge to the a main blockchain such as Bitcoin or Ethereum, often to solve problems of the main blockchain such as transaction speed and high gas fees. Polygon and Tether are sidechains of Ethereum for example.

SIMP / SIMPING

Someone who tries way too hard to impress a person, typically an NFT creator simps an NFT whale.

SMART CONTRACT
a computer program or a transaction protocol which is intended to automatically execute, control or document legally relevant events and actions according to the terms of a contract. Smart contracts increase transparency and trust, as the transaction is immutable (it can't be disputed or changed) and no third-party intermediaries are needed to complete it. Bitcoin doesn't have native smart contract capability.

SMFH
Shaking My Fucking Head, typically said to a stupid person.

SMH
Shaking my head

SOCK PUPPET
a scam account used to lure investors into scams and fake investment opportunities.

SOFT FORK
a protocol update of a blockchain that is backward-compatible, which means that nodes that do not upgrade to newer versions will still see the chain as valid.

SR
Super Rare, a NFT marketplace where artist sell 1/1 art.

STABLECOIN
a cryptocurrency where the price is pegged to fiat money (Dollar) or a commodity such as gold in order to create less volatility. USDC, USDT and DAI are examples for stable coins.

STAKING
a process to lock up a specific amount of cryptocurrency to earn for a specifiy APY (or APR = Annual Percentage Rate) rewards in the same cryptocurrency. The longer the crypto is staked, the greater the reward. Staking will support the price of a cryptocurrency.

STFU
Shut The Fuck Up

SZN
Season, in the meaning of a market cycle (bear of bull)

T **TBF**
To Be Frank

TBH
To be honest

TESTNET
is a test blockchain for developers.

TETHER
is an ERC-20 stablecoin, pegged 1:1 to the US Dollar (currency symbol USDT). It is used to get in and out of certain cryptocurrencies in trading strategies.

Do not buy USDT as a long term investment, as it will never raise in value against the US dollar! Tether is issues by a company in Hongkong and has not been audited up to day how they back up their coin.

TICKER SYMBOL

letters assigned to describe a stock, for example "AAPL" for Apple Inc or "KO" for The Coca Cola Company.

TINA

There Is No Alternative, as in response to the question "why are you investing in Bitcoin?"

TOKEN SWAP

direct exchange between one token and another or from one exchange to another.

TRANSACTION FEE

a fee to process transactions on a blockchain (see GAS)

TOKENIZE

a process to turn an asset into a digital value.

TRUSTLESS

Where there is no centralized control – decentralization

TWITTER

Web 2.0 social media platform used extensively by the crypto and NFT community.

TY

Thank You

TYSM / TYVM

Thank You So Much / Thank You Very Much

U UNISWAP

one of the most popular decentralized crypto trading protocols (DEX) where you can exchange and trade different ERC-20 tokens on Ethereum. They are governed by holders of the Uniswap Protocol token (UNI).

UNSTOPPABLE DOMAINS

name of a US company that offers web3 domain names.

USDC

is like TETHER (USDT) a stablecoin pegged 1:1 with the US Dollar available on the Ethereum blockchain. The Centre Consortium, based in the US, is running this stable coin and was founded the peer-to-peer payment services company Circle and the cryptocurrency exchange Coinbase.

V VOLATILE/VOLATILITY

when a market prices rapidly move up and down within a short amount of time, causing many leveraged crypto derivative traders to get REKT.

W WAGMI

We Are Going to Make It! Expression used when buying into a position, hoping to get rich.

WALLET
a place to store your cryptocurrency and tokens. See chapter 2 in our Ultimate NFT Guide book.

WAMI
We Already Made It

WDYT
What Do You Think?

WEAK HANDS
see PAPER HANDS.

WEB 1.0
the internet web from around 1990 to 2005, also known as the read-only web.

WEB 2.0
the internet web, from 2005 to the present, also known as the read-write web, dominated by social media platforms like Facebook and Google. In Web 2.0 many content producers are unhappy that only a few mega-corporations dominate the vast majority of websites.

WEB 3.0
A proposed new, but not yet realized concept for the internet, which is characterized by decentralization, the absence of a single body of control, and censorship. It will take several more years before it comes. The idea is to take away the power of the big tech companies and hand it back to the individual. Central to Web 3.0 technology is the blockchain.

WEN
When

WEN MOON
Short for "When moon?" – meaning when will the price finally shoot upwards?

WETH / wETH
is a wrapped ETH that has 1:1 value of ETH, but has more features and is useful when making multiple offers on marketplaces like Opensea.

WGMI
We gonna make it.

WHALE
a person who holds large amounts of a coin (usually Bitcoin or Ethereum) or NFTs. A whale holds so many coins/tokens that he or she can influence the market price when selling or buying aggressively. An NFT whale is for example Pranksy on Twitter. A bitcoin whale is Grayscale Bitcoin Trust (GBTC).

WHITEPAPER
a document published by a crypto or NFT project that gives potential investors technical information about its concept. It often includes a roadmap for how it plans to grow.

WIFE CHANGING
life changing, as in "this is life changing money!"

WRAPPED ETH
see WETH

WHITELIST / ALLOWLIST
a list of handpicked users (email or wallet addresses) that are given early access to purchase NFTs from a collection before the project is publicly available. This group can usually mint at a cheaper price or for gas fee only.

Y **YODO**
You only die once. The opposite of YOLO, as in "Don't buy that shitcoin dude, yodo!".

YOLO
You only live once, as in "Let's buy that shitcoin, yolo!"

Z **ZERO-KNOWLEDGE PROOF**
a method in cryptography (also called "zero-knowledge protocol") by which one party (the prover) can prove to another party (the verifier) that a given statement is true without revealing it.

Resources

[1] https://www.rolandberger.com/en/Insights/Publications/Tokenization-The-future-of-financial-markets.html

[2] https://www.theverge.com/tldr/2021/3/17/22336115/charmin-nft-toilet-paper-cryptoart-marketing

[3] https://www.investopedia.com/terms/b/blockchain.asp

[4] https://www.techtarget.com/searchsecurity/news/252521775/Paige-Thompson-found-guilty-in-2019-Capital-One-data-breach

[5] https://www.zdnet.com/finance/blockchain/europe-votes-to-crack-down-on-anonymous-crypto-transfers/

[6]https://ycharts.com/indicators/ethereum_transactions_per_day#:~:text=Ethereum%20Transactions%20Per%20Day%20is,10.93%25%20from%20one%20year%20ago

[7]https://ycharts.com/indicators/bitcoin_transactions_per_day#:~:text=Bitcoin%20Transactions%20Per%20Day%20is,14.34%25%20from%20one%20year%20ago

[8] https://phemex.com/blogs/crypto-minting-vs-crypto-mining

[9] https://ethereum.org/en/developers/docs/consensus-mechanisms/pos/

[10] https://news.artnet.com/market/attempt-to-flip-nft-first-tweet-flops-2099625

[11] Photo by Pixabay from Pexels: https://www.pexels.com/photo/short-coated-black-and-brown-puppy-in-white-and-red-polka-dot-ceramic-mug-on-green-field-39317/

[12] https://www.nytimes.com/2022/01/26/crosswords/what-is-a-meme.html

[13] https://www.forbes.com/sites/abrambrown/2021/03/03/3lau-nft-nonfungible-tokens-justin-blau/?sh=64c1a05d4643

[14] https://www.coindesk.com/business/2022/02/09/zynga-plans-first-nft-games-web-3-acquisitions-in-2022/

[15] https://finance.yahoo.com/news/15-nft-cases-could-mainstream-164631131.html

[16] https://www.coindesk.com/business/2021/09/30/dolce-gabbanas-first-nft-collection-sells-for-57-m/

[17] https://www.cnbc.com/2018/09/13/about-12-percent-of-people-buying-concert-ticketsget-scammed-.html

[18] https://www.ledgerinsights.com/ipwe-to-launch-nft-platform-for-patents-using-ibm-tech/

[19] https://d2u3kfwd92fzu7.cloudfront.net/Art%20Market%202022.pdf page 36

[20] https://en.wikipedia.org/wiki/Metaverse

[21] https://onlineonly.christies.com/s/beeple-first-5000-days/beeple-b-1981-

1/112924

[22] https://news.artnet.com/market/beeple-everydays-controversy-nft-or-not-1952124

[23] https://decrypt.co/62037/missing-or-stolen-nfts-how-to-protect

[24] https://docs.ipfs.tech/concepts/what-is-ipfs/

[25] https://www.makeuseof.com/interplanetary-file-system-persistent-web/

[26] https://news.artnet.com/market/over-50-percent-of-art-is-fake-130821

[27] https://news.artnet.com/art-world/recent-art-forgery-scandals-705428

[28] https://www.vanityfair.com/culture/2012/10/wolfgang-beltracchi-helene-art-scam

[29] https://www.canvasgallery.com/blog/most-notorious-art-forgeries/

[30] https://www.itstartswithadam.com/blog/what-is-an-art-connoisseur

[31] https://www.youtube.com/watch?v=ygufyC4v2XE

[32] https://en.wikipedia.org/wiki/Who_the_$%26%25_Is_Jackson_Pollock%3F

[33] https://www.phoenixnewtimes.com/news/who-the-and-is-jackson-pollock-6644555

[34] https://www.theartnewspaper.com/1998/11/01/exploitation-of-the-tate-archives-trial-of-accused-paintings-fraudster

[35] https://techcrunch.com/2020/03/25/the-future-of-collectibles-is-digital/

[36] https://blog.hobbydb.com/2016/04/16/how-big-are-the-collectible-markets/

[37] https://archives.fbi.gov/archives/news/stories/2005/july/operation-bullpen-overview

[38] http://www.vam.ac.uk/content/articles/a/computer-art-history/

[39] https://time.com/nextadvisor/investing/cryptocurrency/ethereum-price-history/

[40] https://en.wikipedia.org/wiki/CryptoKitties

[41] https://theculturetrip.com/north-america/usa/new-york/new-york-city/articles/andy-warhol-and-his-artistic-influence/

[42] https://www.warhol.org/exhibition/warhol-and-the-amiga/

[43] https://coinjournal.net/news/fdic-says-deposit-insurance-does-not-apply-to-crypto/

[44] https://en.wikipedia.org/wiki/Coinbase

[45] https://www.businessinsider.com/coinbase-warning-users-could-lose-crypto-bankruptcy-earnings-2022-5

[46] https://cryptoart.io/data

[47] https://nonfungible.com

[48] https://www.forbes.com/sites/leeorshimron/2022/08/13/axie-infinity-pernicious-pyramid-scheme-or-gaming-breakthrough/?sh=7a88761074b3

[49] https://auction.van-ham.com/en/browse/search_category/NFT_Unikat_51.html

[50] https://www.one37pm.com/nft/justin-aversano-twin-flames-nft-photography

[51] https://news.cryptorank.io/recent-performance-of-top-10-nft-collections-by-market-cap/
[52] https://coincentral.com/nft-derivative-projects-guide-official-vs-unofficial-derivatives/
[53] https://nftscores.io/how-to-get-whitelist-spots-for-upcoming-nfts/
[54] https://findstack.com/nft-statistics/
[55] https://www.nftgators.com/european-union-wants-to-fight-counterfeiting-and-forgery-with-nfts/
[56] https://www.forbes.com/profile/vitalik-buterin
[57] https://www.forbes.com/advisor/investing/cryptocurrency/ethereum-2/
[58] https://techcrunch.com/2022/06/23/solana-launches-web3-focused-smartphone-saga-to-improve-crypto-mobile-relationship/
[59] https://www.clearviewsys.com/blog.html?p=getting-to-know-solana-not-your-average-cryptocurrency
[60] https://www.hashkey.com/en/insights/nft-infrastructure-the-next-high-ground-to-seize.html
[61] https://finbold.com/guide/binance-smart-chain/
[62] https://www.cnbc.com/2022/06/14/coinbase-lays-off-18percent-as-execs-prepare-for-recession-crypto-winter.html
[63] https://www.hashkey.com/en/insights/nft-infrastructure-the-next-high-ground-to-seize.html
[64] https://dailycoin.com/chiliz-chz-project-review-recent-developments-future-events-community/
[65] https://www.fool.com/the-ascent/cryptocurrency/articles/up-over-125-heres-why-chiliz-is-smoking-hot-this-month/
[66] https://www.coindesk.com/business/2022/06/22/ebay-acquires-nft-marketplace-knownorigin-for-undisclosed-amount/
[67] https://en.wikipedia.org/wiki/Funko
[68] https://www.hiveblockchain.com/
[69] https://investors.block.xyz/overview/default.aspx
[70] https://investor.canaan-creative.com/
[71] https://www.investopedia.com/terms/e/etf.asp
[72] https://www.cointribune.com/en/news-en/edward-snowden-warns-against-nfts/
[73] https://www.forbes.com/advisor/investing/cryptocurrency/bitcoins-energy-usage-explained/
[74] https://liquidstack.com/crypto-solutions
[75] https://www.genesis-mining.com/
[76] https://blog.ethereum.org/2021/05/18/country-power-no-more/
[77] https://www.iyops.org/post/energy-consumption-cryptocurrency-vs-traditional-banks
[78] https://www.nasdaq.com/articles/research:-bitcoin-consumes-less-than-half-

the-energy-of-the-banking-or-gold-industries
[79] https://www.pressreader.com/usa/chicago-tribune/20220608/282913799138835
[80] https://www.coindesk.com/learn/us-crypto-tax-guide-2022/
[81] https://finbold.com/eu-seeks-to-prohibit-anonymous-crypto-wallets-in-new-aml-regulations/
[82] https://www.investopedia.com/terms/h/howey-test.asp
[83] https://investorjunkie.com/nfts/are-nfts-securities/
[84] https://www.wipo.int/about-ip/en/
[85] https://boardroom.tv/gary-vee-michael-rubin-nft-crash/

Printed in Great Britain
by Amazon

15697144R00129